PRAISE FOR

THE OBJECTIVE OF PROPHECY

Truly awesome! This book is a prophetic voice that has embraced the loving nature of God and the season of grace that Jesus ushered in on the cross. The reader will clearly understand why prophetic judgment is not an option today and why God will not speak in a way that belittles or devalues a believer's life. Every word spoken in the name of God should be spoken in the hot pursuit of love and for lifting our head so we might gaze into the beauty of Father's tender loving eyes.

Jack Frost
Shiloh Place Ministries

Graham Cooke's book, *The Objective of Prophecy*, is destined to be one of the most practical tools the Holy Spirit will use to enrich and deepen the lives of many who desire to move more powerfully in the gift of prophecy. I love the way the book is structured and the very practical applications and readings at the end of the chapters. The sidebars telling the stories of great people in the kingdom of God who moved in prophecy after the apostolic age are a great encouragement to us who do believe God still speaks to His church. I am excited about this series of books that Graham will write. I will encourage its reading by the students at our Global School of Missions, Church Planting and Supernatural Ministry. I consider Graham Cooke one of the most respected persons I know who not only has a prophetic gift but who is also in the office of a prophet. It will be hard to find a more practical book to help you grow in prophecy. Graham has walked through many rough seasons in his life, and I am proud to watch him live out his life with great integrity and faithfulness to the author of all prophecy. Graham has been faithful to continue to bear the testimony of Jesus, which is the spirit of prophecy.

Randy Clark
Global Awakening

Once again, Graham Cooke delivers an extraordinary book on prophecy. His unique ability to communicate spiritual truth is refreshingly authentic and theologically sound. As one who ministers in the prophetic, I am indebted to the wisdom of years that Graham has put into this writing. *The Objective of Prophecy* is truly a one-of-a-kind manuscript that reveals the heart and mind of one of the foremost prophets and thinkers in the church today. It is a must-read that will help you navigate through the deep waters of prophetic ministry.

Larry Randolph
Larry Randolph Ministries

I highly recommend Graham's new book. He has profound insights into the nature of the prophetic ministry and never loses sight of the practical application.

Jack Deere
Evangelical Foundation Ministries

Graham Cooke's writings and teachings always leave me hungering and thirsting for more—more of God, more divine revelation, more understanding of God's heart, ways and values. His writings whet my appetite for the deep things of the Spirit because the truths Graham presents come alive within my heart. *The Objective of Prophecy* is full of divinely inspired revelatory treasures—treasures that took years of searching, refining, and preparing to bring them as gifts to you, the reader. The richness of its contents reveals that the writer has truly paid a great price to pen its pages. I love this book!

Patricia King
Extreme Prophetic

In *The Objective of Prophecy*, Graham Cooke has clearly articulated truth that is attainable and achievable. He demonstrates what is possible for those who are concerned to grow churches that announce and demonstrate the kingdom of God. Graham provides practical and incisive insight that releases a congregation to move forward together into who they are called to be. There is absolutely no doubt that this book will both initiate the way forward and build the future for churches that are intent on cultivating an appetite for God.

Peter McHugh
Senior Minister, C3Centre

I had hardly advanced into the first chapter when I ran smack into a classic Graham Cooke revelation. He wrote, "God is more interested in creating collaborative prophetic communities than He is in birthing a new generation of prophetic superstars." If this is so (and I think it is), then God will surely use this new book as a tool to shape the skills and disposition of a new generation of prophetic voices. This new generation will have the ability to collaborate with one another and the throne room in a manner that will build a canopy of agreement between heaven and earth. Asaph taught his musician sons how to flow in the prophetic anointing of David's tabernacle, and I believe Graham's counsel will tune the instruments of the sons and daughters that God is raising to flow in the prophetic tabernacle that covers us in these last days.

Lance Wallnau
Lancelearning Group

I received a new level of faith in the prophetic reading this book. Graham reveals the intentionality of God's love and encouragement toward us and makes it clear how we are to hear His voice, know His heart, and prophesy confidently.

Julie Anderson
Prayer for the Nations

There is a curious tendency in "Spirit-filled" church life to promote the giftings of the New Covenant Spirit in the context of what is really Old Covenant practice. No wonder that we struggle with certain anomalies. However, there is brilliant news! Graham Cooke's new book, *The Objective of Prophecy*, is a significant and mature contribution to the prophetic teaching arena, and his approach is best summarized by his comment, "Any time someone receives a prophetic word, grace should explode in his heart." Well said! The rest of the book is consistent with that statement in both its well-developed content and easily implemented practical exercises. This book is worthy of wide endorsement and exposure. We need a healthy, life-giving approach to the understanding and practice of prophecy, and Graham manages to accomplish this extremely well.

David Crabtree
Senior Pastor, DaySpring Church, Sydney, Australia

I've always enjoyed Graham's writings and public ministry. His recent bite-size, interactive format is just in time for a faster thinking, activational, and demanding generation. He makes me think and take time to pause with insights that act as keys, unlocking my own creativity. Keep those keys coming—let's see what treasures lie ahead!

Steve Witt
Edify Ministries International
Author of *Experiencing Father's Embrace*

It's rare to find a prophet who can prophesy *and* train other to do the same! Graham's new book puts a rich treasure into the hands of the church, not just to understand the nature of the prophetic, but to develop a sensitive heart to the voice of God. When Graham first came to CFC 16 years ago, he prophesied many things that we are now walking in. But he also empowered us to develop the prophetic when he left. If you can't get Graham to come and visit you personally, then this book is a very close second! It imparts God's heart, has wonderful insights, is easily understood, and at the same time gives very practical instructions on how to develop the prophetic. I doubt if there is a better book on the prophetic in print.

Paul Reid
Leader, Life Link Team, Christian Fellowship Church, Belfast

In Graham Cooke's new book, *The Objective of Prophecy*, he outdoes himself, as I've come to expect. He continually amazes me with each line in this book. How can one man come up with so many quotable quotes? Wow! Based solely on Scripture yet lived out in his own life, the content of Graham's new book will walk you through the real purpose for prophecy today. This book is about transition in the prophetic gift currently operating and accepted within the church. So, use this as a primer for yourself, your friends, or even your own church group. You will never think of prophecy in the same way again!

Steve Shultz
The Elijah List

My personal acquaintance with this author makes my endorsement to be both a privilege and a responsibility. There are few voices in the realm of the prophetic dimension in which there would be the freedom to recommend a manuscript without reserve. Graham Cooke is one that has excelled in this needed realm. He has been given an unusual ability to remain biblically accurate and spiritually insightful while wrapping every instruction and expectation in the love of the Father. If your heart hungers to know and become involved in the prophetic dimension, don't hesitate to make this volume your very own.

Bob Mumford
Lifechangers

VOLUME THREE

THE OBJECTIVE
of PROPHECY

RELEASING THE PROPHETIC POWER TO RESTORE

Graham Cooke

THE PROPHETIC EQUIPPING SERIES

The Objective of Prophecy was formerly known as Approaching the Heart of Prophecy, MODULE THREE.

BRILLIANT BOOK HOUSE

Brilliant Book House LLC
PO Box 871450
Vancouver, WA 98687
www.brilliantbookhouse.com

Requests for information should be addressed to:
Email: admin@brilliantperspectives.com

Unless otherwise indicated, all Scripture quotations are taken from The Holy Bible, New American Standard Version. Copyright © 1960, 1962, 1963, 1971, 1972, 1973, 1975, 1977, 1995 by The Lockman Foundation.

ISBN: 978-1-7358706-0-1

DEDICATION

I have many friends around the world, people who are dedicated to the King and His kingdom. They have gone through much and emerged through it to be loving, gentle, kind, and humble with a joy that empowers them to live from delight.

They are seekers, warriors, dreamers, planners, architects of what church would look like *if* it practiced kingdom living.

They have paid a price for where they are but never talk about it. They narrate the story of what God did in them and who He became to them in the course of growing into great leaders and powerful ministries.

I am so proud to know you.

ACKNOWLEDGMENTS

People who don't quit are the only ones who can leave a legacy worth following.

I am amazed at the quality of people whom God has put around my life—people who lived in the shadows where the poor people walk. Those who passed out of this world unremarked and unknown, save by the One who never forgets a labor of love.

People who fought and persisted for one small victory after another until something emerged out of the battlefield that resembled more a high tower of safety than a meeting place.

All those who took on the local giants of uncaring, inneffective government; the politics of care that waste fortunes; the inanity of religious voices that never stop speaking but who declare nothing.

We are all ever, only challenged by the goodness of the One who lives within us and is Himself magnificent, indomitable, and wonderfully cheerful.

Kudos to Him and to all who work alongside Him in hellish places.

TABLE OF CONTENTS

INTRODUCTION

And it shall come to pass afterward that I will pour out My Spirit on all flesh; your sons and your daughters shall prophesy, your old men shall dream dreams, your young men shall see visions. And also on My menservants and My maidservants I will pour out My Spirit in those days. (Joel 2:28–29)

THE WORLD CHANGED THE DAY the Holy Spirit fell on Jesus' remaining disciples in that famed upper room in Jerusalem. The Spirit of God, reserved in the Old Testament for a select few, had now been placed on anyone who sought and loved Christ. With that outpouring came the gifts of the Spirit. While once only a few could prophesy, suddenly everyone could.

I have been in the prophetic ministry since 1974. I began prophesying the year before. That's more than thirty years of sharing the love God has placed in my heart. Amazingly, I'm still learning—and I never want to stop. Every year, I understand something new about God and His ways. He never ceases to intrigue me.

More than a decade ago, my book *Developing Your Prophetic Gifting* was first published. It has been a greater success than I could have ever imagined. It has gone through many re-printings; several publishers have taken it up; it has been written in many, many languages; and it still is on the best-seller list; and yet the material I teach now is light years beyond that original manuscript. I have come a long way in the years since I wrote that first book. For one thing, I have taught countless prophetic schools during that time. As I work with students and emerging prophetic voices, I have had my own gift shaped and honed. "As iron sharpens iron, so a man sharpens the countenance of his friend," as it says in Proverbs 27:17. The people I have met have pushed me further into the things of the prophetic. They have challenged me to find fresh ways of equipping, explaining, and encouraging.

For several months, I have felt the Lord prompt me to rewrite *Developing Your Prophetic Gifting*, adding the material I have taught in my schools over the past ten years since it was published. This book is the first in a series of six that will more fully equip people longing to speak the words of God to those around them.

Following the unqualified success of the spirituality journals in the Being with God Series,[1] I have decided to develop this material into the same format.

Each book has assignments, exercises, and meditations that, if followed, will bring each individual into an experience of God within the context of the material.

Together, we will study the practical elements of hearing God, of moving in the Spirit, of knowing God's nature, and of representing

A SMALL MIND IS INCOMPATIBLE WITH A BIG HEART

His heart to someone else. We will learn how to be grounded in the love, grace, and rhythm of God. It is my prayer that these books will give you something fresh about who God wants to be for you. As you read the principles and illustrations within, I pray that you will be excited and inspired to venture further into what God has for you.

Prophecy comes when we have a burden to encourage and bless the people around us. There is no magic formula to prophesying; it all depends on our love for God. When we love Him fully, that love should

---

1   See www.brilliantbookhouse.com for more information.

spill over onto the people around us. Prophecy is simply encouraging, exhorting, and comforting people by tuning them in to what God has for them. In every church in the world, there are people who need that life-giving word from God. These aren't just the individuals who are obviously struggling; some appear to have everything together. But God knows what's really going on.

Everyone could benefit from a prophetic word, even those for whom everything is soaring. I love to prophesy over people who are doing really well. If we can target those people and increase their faith at a critical time, they can fly even higher in the things of the Spirit.

New Testament prophecy will be spoken through the context of the gospel of grace. Jesus has received the judgment of God for sin for all those who are living, to enable them to find repentance through the goodness and kindness of God.

Prophecy is now in the context of a family, a company of called-out people who are learning together to become the beloved of God: the bride of Christ. There is a new language in the Spirit to learn and the unity of the Spirit to maintain and enjoy, as a people together.

Of course there are necessary tensions in all good relationships and prophecy is not the way to resolve conflicts. Clearly we need wisdom for those situations.

I believe strongly that the more encouraging, exhorting, and comforting prophecy we have, the better our churches will be. Blessing and encouragement stir up anointing. The more of this kind of prophecy we can have in church, the less we will need intensive, time-consuming pastoral care. People will actually be touched by God and come into the things of the Spirit themselves. Individuals

WHEN THE CHURCH RUNS OUT OF ENCOURAGEMENT, THE WORLD RUNS INTO WICKEDNESS

will realize that, yes, they are loved personally by God. That kind of revelation will stoke up their faith in ways a counseling session never could.

I know I need that kind of encouragement every day from the Holy Spirit. I can't remember the last time I asked Him to encourage me and He didn't. He may not speak it out immediately, but He always meets me at the point of my greatest need. That's just who the Holy Spirit is and what He loves to do.

This book can help you go further in the prophetic than you have ever hoped. After all, *"Eye has not seen, nor ear heard, nor have entered into the heart of man the things which God has prepared for those who love Him"* (1 Corinthians 2:9).

The Objective of Prophecy is not a quick read. I encourage you to take your time going through this book, reading slowly and with your heart, until you understand the themes and thoughts it contains.

Furthermore, don't neglect the exercises, case studies, and Bible readings included at the end of each volume—they are valuable practice tools that will take the lessons taught and put them into practice in your life.

Throughout this book, I have included several sidebar articles about some of my prophetic heroes. These are people who lived after the Bible was finished being written, heard the voice of God for themselves, and did marvelous exploits for the kingdom. I hope this will open your eyes to a few of the people who have gone before us.

I have also included some suggestions of resources that may help you further explore the themes contained in this book. I hope they prompt you to dig deeper into the things of the Spirit.

Blessings on your journey into the prophetic!

Graham

VOLUME THREE

THE OBJECTIVE
of PROPHECY

RELEASING THE PROPHETIC POWER TO RESTORE

<u>VOLUME THREE</u>
The Objective of Prophecy
WHAT YOU WILL LEARN IN THIS SEGMENT:

- Why prophecy is vital in a post-modern world.
- The difference between prophecy and teaching.
- Prophecy releases a personal impartation of the purposes of God.
- The importance of being and the grace of doing.
- Prophecy and humility are irrepressible companions.
- Prophecy restores dignity and self-respect.
- How to edify, comfort, and encourage.
- Releasing correction and warning properly.
- Provide direction and enhance personal vision.
- Complement teaching and confirm the revealed word.
- Release the church into new truth and practice.
- Prophecy provides insight in pastoral situations.
- Produce evangelistic breakthroughs.
- Provide a prayer agenda for individuals and groups.
- Know the difference between the supernatural and the spectacular.
- Understand institutionalized opposition to the prophetic.
- Develop two relationships with God as Abba and Father.
- Childlike trust in the bedrock of mature faith.

THE OBJECTIVE *of* PROPHECY

IMAGINE THE LIFE OF MOSES as he led a million Israelites through forty years in the wilderness. Life could not have been much fun for the man. First, he was openly envied by others for his close relationship with God. Second, he was blamed, despised, criticized, and ridiculed any time a problem cropped up along the way to the Promised Land. The people ran the man ragged. Bread from heaven wasn't enough; they wanted meat. Water from a rock wasn't enough; they wanted more. The law of God itself was resisted.

On top of all of that, Moses was forced to listen to the life issues and difficulties of more than a million people. In each of those cases, he felt compelled to pray and seek out the Lord for His judgment. Such a process would be exhausting for a pastor of a hundred-member church; one can only imagine the strain on Moses.

Fortunately, there were people who loved Moses and whom the prophet trusted. When his father-in-law, Jethro, watched Moses judge cases from dawn to dusk, he was appalled.

"What is this thing that you are doing for the people? Why do you alone sit, and all the people stand before you from morning until evening?" he asked in Exodus 18:14.

"Because the people come to me to inquire of God," Moses replied in verses 15 and 16. *"When they have a difficulty, they come to me, and I judge between one and another; and I make known the statutes of God and His laws."*

Jethro, an outsider who had just arrived in the Israelite camp, saw a pattern in the constant stream of questions and answers that Moses endured, and proposed a plan. He told his son-in-law to record the problems and answers he had already faced so they could be used as a precedent for others to judge what was going on. With such material in hand, Moses could appoint deputies to deal with those complaints using the prophet's own words and answers. Moses, meanwhile, could preside over new situations, listening and providing the word of the Lord. Thousands of years later, our court systems use the same principle of precedence as Jethro laid out.

Jethro's wisdom probably saved Moses' life, leadership, and sanity. The children of Israel learned to interact with and interpret the written, or revealed, Word of God, and the new word given by Moses through prophetic utterance. This pattern still exists today. The present-day Church has the revealed Word of God in Scripture, which allows us to understand and follow God's ways. We can be grounded in the Bible and able to determine the heart and will of God for ourselves.

When we encounter situations that don't appear to have a clear precedent or answer in Scripture, we may need to access the prophetic ministry. This gift will echo the Bible faithfully, drive us to the feet of

THE KINGDOM OF HEAVEN IS PRESENT-FUTURE, THEREFORE...

Jesus, and never usurp our will or force us into unsound judgments or actions.

I teach my prophetic students to always keep one question at the forefront of their minds when they are asked for a word: "Is this person's need best served by an increased understanding of Scripture, or do they need a *now* word, aligned with Scripture, that will personalize God's Word in a way that increases faith and confidence and releases them from hindrances and bondage?" When we discern that God's answer for their need is obviously contained in Scripture, we should refer them to a teacher who has the gift to exposit that precedent to them.

The Bible clearly distinguishes between prophecy and teaching. It emphasizes that both prophetic and teaching gifts exist and that the two have separate functions with the common goal of growing people into spiritual maturity. *"He Himself gave some to be apostles, some prophets, some evangelists, and some pastors and teachers,"* the apostle Paul wrote in Ephesians 4:11. Paul went even further in 1 Corinthians 12:27–31:

> *Now you are the body of Christ, and members individually. And God has appointed these in the church: first apostles, second prophets, third teachers, after that miracles, then gifts of healings, helps, administrations, varieties of tongues. Are all apostles? Are all prophets? Are all teachers? Are all workers of miracles? Do all have gifts of healings? Do all speak with tongues? Do all interpret? But earnestly desire the best gifts.*

Both prophecy and teaching are needed in the Church. One does not have precedence over the other; it is not our preference or prejudice that determines which gift we should use, but rather the demands of the situation we find ourselves in. Prophecy and teaching have different goals, and both are vital if we are to understand God's ways.

...IT REQUIRES A PROPHETIC PEOPLE TO ESTABLISH ITS RULE

THE DIFFERENCE BETWEEN
TEACHING AND PROPHECY

While teaching allows us to gain a full understanding of God's principles for life, prophecy imparts the purpose of God in our current situation. Teaching reveals to us the mind of God, while prophecy deals with His heart. God, like us, both thinks and feels. *"But I am poor and needy; yet the LORD thinks upon me,"* says Psalm 40:17. *"Jesus wept,"* records John 11:35. Christ both thinks about us and feels for us.

God loves to express His heart toward us and make His thoughts plain. Those feelings will never countermand Scripture, which is profitable for our teaching, correction, reproof, and exhortation (see 2 Timothy 3:16). In fact, it was the Holy Spirit-inspired word of the prophets that enabled the heroes of our faith to write Scripture in the first place. One could argue that by believing in the Bible, we automatically believe in prophecy! We cannot separate the two on any level. *"For prophecy never came by the will of man, but holy men of God spoke as they were moved by the Holy Spirit,"* says 2 Peter 1:21.

Many people rightly worry that an over-dependence on experience, at the expense of the solid grounding in the Word that good teaching builds, may lead to error and abuse. On the flip side of that coin, others are rightly concerned that the ministry of the Word without the spirit of revelation, which the prophetic enhances, can lead to a correct but sterile formality.

All knowledge must lead to an actual experience if our spiritual life is going to develop. Knowledge that fails to capitalize on experience is not worth anything in the spiritual realm. It ensures that our head is filled with instruction that has not progressed to life-changing enlightenment. We are scholars who never graduate because we fail every life test. We know in our head but our heart is untouched. We can quote scripture but we do not encounter the God who breathed it into life.

I know from personal experience that it is possible and beneficial to have both prophets and teachers operating together. After all, that's the way God intended it.

To move in even the simplest prophetic gift requires an understanding of the mind and heart of God and how to release that revelation to others. Prophetic words have different strengths of impact depending on the situation, circumstances, faith level and understanding of the receiver, and also the ability, experience, understanding, and relationship of the giver to the Holy Spirit.

Prophecy is a gift of the Holy Spirit; it does not belong to people. The Spirit gives gifts at His own discretion. Anyone can be used in the gift of prophecy provided they believe and have accepted Jesus Christ as their Savior, are filled with the Holy Spirit, and are open to moving in the supernatural.

Knowing that all Spirit-filled Christians can prophesy does not make everyone who does a prophet. Prophetic anointing contains various levels and stages, beginning with the shallow end of basic prophecy, encouragement, edification, and comfort. However, moving through levels of prophetic ministry and into the office of a prophet requires considerable training, experience, and development over many years. On average, it takes about twenty years to fully form a prophet, depending on the training, discipling, and mentoring one has received.

WHEN OUR EGO IS SMALL, THE PRESENCE OF GOD IS ENLARGED

A strong, clean, purposeful relationship with God, wedded to a life of prayer, study, and meditation of Scripture, will always be more productive spiritually than a casual familiarity in those areas.

HUMILITY IS THE KEY

One of the most difficult questions for Christians to grapple with is "How do I receive the gift of prophecy?" Unfortunately, even the question is flawed. Prophecy is not for some people more than others. It is not a reward for faithful years of Christian service; it cannot be earned. Prophecy is a gift given freely by the Holy Spirit.

However, the ministry of a prophet is not open to everyone. That is a specific calling and anointing.

We are all required to witness to the unchurched people in our community; that does not make us all evangelists in the fivefold tradition.

We are all expected to give advice, help, and support to one another as an act of lovingkindness and relationship. That does not make us pastors. We can all impart truth and learning in a sharing environment but we are not specifically teachers.

Our Western mindset leads us to believe that *doing* is more important than *being*. We feel as though we always have to be doing something spiritually to earn God's favor: cleaning the church, teaching Sunday school, driving kids to football practice, working late, running errand after errand after errand. But this is not God's desire for us: He only wants to live with, and in, us. He longs for a relationship separate from the work of His kingdom. He wants to *be* with us.

We each carry a profound and unfathomable call on our life, placed there by God Himself. It is fresh and new and completely beyond our natural ability to accomplish—God has called us to do something we cannot possibly do. We can meditate on that call for the rest of our days, strategize it, and even try to seize it; it doesn't matter. Like reaching for the stars, God's call is beyond us. It's a gift God has given each one of His children. In fact, our inability to accomplish it is exactly why He selected us to carry that call: *"But God has chosen the foolish things of the world to put to shame the wise, and God has chosen the weak things of the world to put to shame the things which are mighty,"* Paul wrote in 1 Corinthians 1:27.

The call must be impossible for us so that we can develop a relationship with the Lord that revolves around intimacy and dependency. There is no substitute for a life of joy-filled sensitivity to the person of the Holy Spirit.

Each day we rejoice in the grace of absolute dependence on the name and the nature of the Lord. Our walk with Him is filled with a conscious dependence upon who He is for us now in this present situation. Our hope is in Him. Our confidence rises up to meet His intentional nature.

Inevitably, there will be some people to whom God entrusts the gift of prophecy on a regular basis. Those who are moving in an increase of revelatory anointing can be said to be moving into a prophetic ministry rather than just an extensive use of that gift.

PROPHECY IS A JOY TO GIVE AND TO RECEIVE

When that ministry begins to impact whole cultures, nations, and governments, it signifies the change from prophetic ministry to the office of a prophet.

Prophecy does not make some people better than others—there are no superior or inferior believers. Structural hierarchy has no place in the gifts of the Spirit.

Christians who perform supernatural exploits, or who have been given immense responsibilities within the kingdom, will have built that influence on a solid base of humility and dependence on God. This level of anointing carries with it a deep sensitivity to, and intimacy with, the Holy Spirit. A lack of humility before God produces an absence of sensitivity to the Holy Spirit; this in turn creates a shortage of compassion for people. The loss of humility is one of the great problems in the realm of prophecy today and flies in the face of what is taught throughout Scripture. In fact, the book of Proverbs is full of warnings regarding pride:

Surely He scorns the scornful, but gives grace to the humble. (Proverbs 3:34)

When pride comes, then comes shame; but with the humble is wisdom. (Proverbs 11:2)

A man's pride will bring him low, but the humble in spirit will retain honor. (Proverbs 29:23)

When we allow pride to pollute our relationship with God, we lose momentum and trust. Our top mission in life is to love God with everything in us and to love our neighbor the same way we love ourselves. Such dependence on God and respect for others produces the humility necessary for God to live in us.

THE NINE OBJECTIVES OF PROPHECY

Prophecy is a gift and ministry that we should tirelessly encourage and disciple in our churches. Unfortunately, human nature leads us to fear things we do not understand, and many misconceptions about prophecy arise out of a lack of knowledge and understanding about what it is, how it works, and the way in which it should be released in the local church.

Yet prophecy is too powerful a gift to ignore or treat poorly. It can accomplish a number of marvelous purposes:

- Restore people's dignity and self-respect,
- Edify, encourage, and comfort the Church,
- Bring correction or warning,
- Provide direction and enhance vision,
- Open up the teaching of the Word and confirm preaching,
- Release the Church into new doctrine or practices,
- Provide insight into counseling situations,
- Provide evangelistic breakthroughs, and
- Provide an agenda for prayer.

PROPHECY RESTORES PEOPLE'S
DIGNITY AND SELF-RESPECT

Many Christians sit in their churches, week after week, with no idea of their own worth and value to the Lord. The enemy, and life in general, conspire to strip people of their God-given identities and concepts of self-worth. For example, many people find it difficult to establish a relationship

PROPHECY DECLARES THE BEAUTY THAT GOD SEES

with God as their Father due to their own poor experience with their family.

Hurts, wounds, rejection, and emotional trauma are a part of our lives, both before and after salvation. Fortunately, we serve a God who is committed to our physical, emotional, and mental healing. His goal is to bring us into the fullness of life in the Spirit. He sees us very differently than we see ourselves: *"The precious sons of Zion, valuable as fine gold, how they are regarded as clay pots, the work of the hands of the potter!"* (Lamentations 4:2).

Prophecy is a wonderful part of that healing and renewing process. When the angel of the Lord visited Gideon in Judges 6, he called out the hidden treasure in the Israelite: *"The LORD is with you, you mighty man of valor!"* The Lord looked beyond Gideon's circumstances—and the fact that he was cowering in a winepress for fear of being taken by the enemy—and started renewing his self-image. The human thing to do would have been to slap Gideon down for being a coward. But God had a better plan and spoke to his potential. The next day, that scared kid pulled down a village stronghold and turned people back to the one true God. When we speak nobility to a person, nobility emerges. If we speak the life of Christ to someone, the life of Christ rises up in them. Prophecy brings us, by direct verbal communication, into contact with God's real perspective on our lives and current situations.

In this context, the goal of prophecy is to open our eyes to God's love and care, enabling us to come to our senses and escape from any snare in which the enemy has tried to entrap us. Prophecy reminds us, in a forthright and loving way, of everything God has provided in Christ Jesus. Prophecy restores our soul, renews our mind, and revives our spirit. Like a cold drink on a hot day, it refreshes us.

Such a prophetic word cuts through the darkness, bringing real light, faith, and confidence. It counters our poor attitudes and negative concepts about ourselves. When Gideon protested God's word, *"Indeed my clan is the weakest in Manasseh, and I am the least in my father's house,"* God just laughed: *"Surely I will be with you, and you shall defeat the Midianites as one man."* God helped Gideon understand and appreciate his personal value.

GOODNESS IS GOD'S THEME AND PERSONALITY, SO IT MUST BE OURS TOO

PROPHECY EDIFIES, ENCOURAGES, AND COMFORTS THE CHURCH

In 1 Corinthians 14:3, the apostle Paul wrote one of the most famous verses on prophecy. *"But he who prophesies speaks edification and exhortation and comfort to men,"* he explained. Often, these are words that explain a part of God's nature in a specific situation. For example, if a prophetic word speaks of the greatness, the majesty, and the supremacy of God, it can stir up the Church to fight, stand its ground, and enter into prevailing prayer and warfare. It has exhorted people to stand firm.

If a word relates to God's compassion, His wholesale forgiveness, and His willingness to extend mercy and cleansing, it will cause people to approach Him and rebuild their lives. It has edified their spirits and released the kind of faith that the Holy Spirit can work with and build on.

Prophecy will not leave the Church feeling confused, degraded, or condemned. It will not make people feel inferior or intimidated. Instead,

SAINT COLUMBA

LIVED: 521 to 597

PROPHETIC SYNOPSIS: Banished from Ireland for his role in starting a war, Columba sailed to the Scottish island of Iona and set up a mission there. The Scots loved him and quickly adopted him as their own. He was a gifted teacher, healer, and prophet. The Holy Spirit would make the saint sound the same to the listener in the front row of his church as he did to someone 1,000 steps away. Once, near Inverness and the fortress of King Brude, he was chanting with monks while Druids tried to distract the crowd with their own songs. Columba came to the walls and sang out Psalm 45:1. His voice was as loud as thunder—the king and the crowd jumped in fear. The Druids ran away.

He was incredibly gifted in prophesying blessing on people. On one occasion, a despised young boy, known in the community for being completely rebellious, snuck up on the saint. As the boy reached out to touch him, Columba grabbed him and pulled him close. Everyone around him said, "Send him away, send him away; why hold on to this wretched and disrespectful boy?" The child was terrified; he shook in Columba's arms.

"Let him be, brothers, just let him be," Columba said. "My son, open your mouth and put out your tongue. Although now this boy seems contemptible to you and quite without worth, yet let no one despise him on that account. For from this hour he not only will not displease you but will find great favor with you, and he will steadily grow from day to day in good conduct and in the virtues of the soul. Wisdom, too, and good sense will increase in him more and more from this day, and in this community of yours he will be a man of high achievement. His tongue also will be gifted with eloquence from God to teach the doctrine of salvation." That boy was Ernene, who became a well-known leader in the Irish church.

KEY COMMENT: "o Lord, grant us that love which can never die, which will enkindle our lamps but not extinguish them, so that they may shine in us and bring light to others."

MORE: Read *The Life of Columba* by Adamnan.

Source: Saint Adamnan, *Life of St Coumba / Adomnán of Iona*, translated by Richard Sharpe (Harmondsworth, Middlesex, England; New York: Penguin Books, 1995).

it will strengthen the ties between God and His people. The word "edi-fication" means "building up," "strengthening," or "improving."

Encouragement is also released by prophecy. At the right time, in the right way, and with the proper word, the Lord can release a magnificent blessing through prophecy. This type of word gives a significant boost to the Church; it will reassure, inspire, and incite people to thanks-giving. It will stimulate faith and create a sense of well-being in the congregation. Put simply, prophecy changes the atmosphere, opening the doors to miracles by injecting faith into people.

Many years ago, I led a conference in a church that mistrusted the supernatural gifts—especially prophecy. The suspicion and unbelief in the room were almost tangible. I knew that unless God moved and did something superb, the weekend would be very difficult.

To prepare, I did the only thing I could do—I rested in the Lord. I resisted the temptation to try to move in the spectacular; instead, I wanted to let the Spirit move in the supernatural. I put all of my energy into being quiet and restful before God, choosing to let my vision be filled up with Him, rather than focusing on my circumstances. When the enemy tries to push anointed ministries into the spectacular, we must resist by humbling ourselves. *"He must increase, but I must decrease"* was how John the Baptist explained it in John 3:30. We are not here to prove how powerful we are, but merely to serve the Lord.

As the weekend started, I knew I couldn't react to the unbelief and negativity. My job was to be still and very aware of the Lord.

There is a difference between the supernatural and the spectacular. The supernatural is God breaking into our time/space world in a way that is astonishing and amazing in its effect on our hearts and lives. Bodies are healed; miracles (producing something out of nothing) occur, which leaves us breathless with amazement; the effect of God on our lives on days can be stunning.

That's the point. The *effect* of God is astonishing. The outcome of His work in our lives leaves us with a sense of wonder. However, mostly His entrance and His appearance can be unobtrusive, modest, quiet, and restrained.

Isaiah knew Him as "the God who hides Himself" (45:15).

Jesus was present to the disciples but hidden from them on the road to Emmaus (see Luke 24). God chose a Bethlehem to reveal Jesus when a Jerusalem would have worked just as well. Elijah discovered that God was not in the wind that could break rocks into pieces. Nor was He in the earthquake or the mighty raging fire (see 1 Kings 19). He was in the whisper of sound, like a gentle breeze blowing—a sound so small only a restful, quiet person could hear it. Stillness is so vital in the prophetic gift and ministry.

Without stillness prophetic people can be tempted to make a show, to do something for effect. The difference between the supernatural and the spectacular is in the cause and effect. With God the supernatural is mostly evidenced after He has moved, as in the parting of the Red Sea (see Exodus 14:21). There was a strong east wind that worked all night turning the sea into dry land. God mostly works unseen, even when He announces Himself!

The spectacular puts on a show up front—lots of hype, showmanship, rhetoric, and bluster. People put on a ringmaster type voice and become the stadium announcer to the audience. The word sounds good but when you write it down

IF YOU CAN DECREASE, GOD WILL INCREASE IN YOU

SAINT AIDAN

Lived: 600 *(estimated)* to 651

Prophetic Synopsis: When King Oswald sent for help to evangelize his kingdom in AD 635, Aidan answered the call. He traveled across Britain and set up a community on the holy island of Lindisfarne. Aidan loved the Northumbrian people, walking all over northern England, preaching the gospel and healing the sick. As the venerable Bede wrote, "He took pains never to neglect anything that he had learned from the writings of the apostles and prophets, and he set himself to carry them out with all his powers."

Aidan was helped by Oswald, who often traveled with the little monk, interpreting for his people. Aidan and Oswald built churches throughout Northumbria. Aidan "cultivated peace and love, purity and humility," wrote Bede.

He was a significantly prophetic man. One Easter, Oswald and Aidan were sitting down to a feast in Oswald's castle. A servant came to Oswald and told him there were several poor people sitting hungry outside the wall. Oswald ordered the food to be taken to the poor and a silver dish broken into pieces to give them spending money. "Why should these fast while I am feasting?" Oswald said. "God loves all alike, and not less the poor, but rather more." Aidan was so touched by Oswald's act that he grabbed the king's hand and said, "May this hand never perish!" Three hundred years later, when Oswald's body was moved from its original burial site, monks found his hand was still perfect.

On another occasion, a man named Utta asked him for a blessing for his boat trip to Denmark. Aidan prophesied that a storm would strike his ship and gave him a bottle of holy oil to keep him safe. Sure enough, when the storm was at its worst, Utta poured the oil into the sea. Even as the sailors screamed, "Lost! Lost! Lost! We'll die," the oil hit the sea and the storm stopped.

Key Comment: "The love of Christ — that wins and conquers all."

More: Read *The Ecclesiastical History of the English People* by Bede

Source: Bede, *The Ecclesiastical History of the English People; The Greater Chronicle; Bede's Letter to Egbert*, eds Judith McClure and Roger Collins (Oxford, NY: Oxford University Press, 1994).

later, the content is actually quite minimal. The presentation can be dazzling and the aftermath disappointing.

The one thing that is visible is the prophet! All we have done is encountered someone's individual anointing rather than being engaged by the living God. Under pressure, prophetic people can try to pull something out of the hat themselves to make something happen. "Fake it till you make it." Cause people to think that God is on the move.

The Lord doesn't work that way. He is normal, humble, gentle, and, mostly, not loud (He has His moments!). He works simply, quietly, honestly, and directly. Often you only know He has been there by the result, the miracle that has occurred. Heaven is not a three-ring circus. God makes a show of the enemy, seldom Himself (see Colossians 2:15). The best prophecy that has the most effect and excellent content is delivered quietly and humbly, even in the presence of thousands of people. It occurs because the prophet is only aware of God and the person who is receiving a word; all else disappears. Real prophets are not crowd-conscious but God-responsive. They engage with the intentionality of God both in the words and the manner in which they can be presented that will do the most good.

In the first meeting, as I stood to teach, God gave me a vision and prophetic interpretation for one of the young men present. In my spirit, I saw the man's father driving a yellow truck. The Lord showed me what company he worked for and the depot where he was based. I told the boy he could find his father there and that the Lord was doing a work of reconciliation. I told the boy quietly and very matter-of-factly. I wanted to be conscious of his feelings and how the Father would speak to him in a crowd. The church went wild! Apparently, the young man had recently accepted Christ, and the church had been praying that God would allow him to meet his father, whom he had not seen since he was four years old.

Talk about an encouragement for that church! The spontaneous applause showed how hungry they were for the hope of Christ to be revealed to them. The Lord did not want to focus on the church's unbelief, instead choosing to move in the opposite spirit. He did something that made their faith explode. That one prophetic word blew the weekend wide open for the supernatural presence of God to come in and change people. Faith began to rise; individuals began to understand that the Lord was mighty and powerful and involved with them. The young man followed up on the prophetic word and has since reconciled with his father. It has born incredible fruit.

Because prophecy so powerfully encourages us, it naturally sparks a spirit of thanksgiving and praise. It can reveal to people exactly what is on God's heart now and what we should do next in response to the moving of the Spirit. While I was speaking at a conference many years ago, the Lord

PROPHECY PROVOKES THANKSGIVING

showed me there was a woman in the auditorium who had been fasting and praying for her unsaved daughter. He told me that this mother was desperately concerned that her rebellious daughter would get into drug-related problems or be taken advantage of sexually.

As I prayed for her, the Lord gave me the prophetic assurance that He was actively involved in this girl's life and that she would come to no harm. Furthermore, the prophetic word told the mother that God had heard her prayers and was moving to answer them. In response to that, the prophecy continued, the mother was to stop praying and begin giving thanks, praising God for His involvement.

For several months afterward, the mother gave thanks and praised God. In the first few weeks, very little changed for the positive — in fact, the situation worsened considerably. Still, the mother held on to the prophetic word and continued in praise and gratitude to the Lord.

God did exactly what He said He was going to do. The daughter has been fully restored to the Lord and her family, and the mother's life has been changed too. She now has a spirit of thanksgiving and a grateful heart. She is a woman who knows how to be released in praise and worship and is a catalyst to lead others to do the same.

God's blessing should propel us into thanksgiving — our excitement over what He is doing must manifest itself in gratitude. Thankfulness is a test we need to pass every day of our lives. Whether life is good or bad, we always have something to give thanks for.

Every church will face tests of character, integrity, and commitment to God and one another. These tests are a vital part of corporate growth and development. If we fail them, we lose vital ground in the realm of the Spirit.

The Church will face many barriers, hindrances, and obstructions as the enemy tries to move us away from our corporate identity and vision, reduce our expectancy for the supernatural, and eliminate any active faith from our community's lifestyle. Discouragement will constantly nip at our heels. When we enter seasons like this, we must release the prophetic amongst the congregation or send for a prophet to help us.

Encouragement in prophecy releases God's perspective and brings confidence and hope. The Western understanding of hope has devalued it — true hope is absolute confidence in God. This type of confidence is at rest in turmoil because it laughs at the actions of the enemy. It produces enough faith that we can stand still and see God — or even march forward in power and expectancy.

Prophecy also releases comfort into lives that have been made bitter by hardness, pain, and difficult circumstances. God does not always shield us from the troubles of life, although He does promise to be with us as we go through those fires. People die for their faith every day. In 2003, some 160,000 people gave their lives for Christ. Loved ones die, children become terminally ill, people's lives are reduced to rubble by unfaithfulness and divorce. Money issues strangle families. Inexplicable tragedy can strike out of the blue.

Into every human tragedy, the Holy Spirit can drop a word of consolation to alleviate pain, reduce stress, invigorate hearts, soothe tension, and provide a wealth of support that will ultimately refresh people and gladden their hearts.

PROPHECY CAN BRING CORRECTION AND WARNING

In Scripture, people were often given warnings through prophetic words and called to repentance and change. In the New Testament the best example of this is found in the letters to seven churches in the book of Revelation, chapters 2 and 3. We will look at just two of these churches, Ephesus and Pergamum.

PROPHETS MUST BE GOOD NEWS, EVEN IF THAT NEWS IS REPENT

Each church was struggling with a particular issue, and the word of prophecy to each was a considerable source of clarity, definition, and strength. When looking at these words, it is helpful to note a similar pattern in each.

First, there is a grace base to corrective prophecy. Second, there is an understanding of the problem. Third, there is the honoring of what is honest and principled. Fourth, there is a clear word spoken directly to the issue. Finally, there is a clear call to repentance and change. Prophecy is always for the common good (see 1 Corinthians 12:7), therefore people must profit from prophecy. A prophet must be good news, even if that news is repent!

To the church at Ephesus there was a call to return to intimacy with the Lord. This is a good, hardworking church, full of perseverance, that has tested false apostles and that is strong in the ways of God. In the midst of all of this, they had slipped away from the first commandment.

Actually this is a common problem amongst churches today where the Great Commission has taken precedence over the First Commandment. In such places, worship is relegated to a minor role and the people are not discipled in a lifestyle of praise, thanksgiving, and rejoicing. Thus there is no intimate connection with the Lord in the hearts of the congregation.

Ephesus used to be excellent in these things but had settled back into a working relationship with the Lord and not a friendship relationship that involved expressions of love and intimacy. In this prophecy there is a clear call to repentance, to think again, and to return to the things they did at first in worship.

The church at Pergamum had been brave enough to plant a church in the heart of the occult district in the city, "where Satan's throne is." They were caught up in the unending struggle between light and darkness. One of their number had been martyred as they constantly faced the battle to speak out for the Lord.

SAINT PATRICK

Lived: 387 to 461

Prophetic Synopsis: Ireland's patron saint was actually English; as a young boy, he was taken as a slave to Ireland. Years later, he escaped back to his homeland, but God had other plans for him.

One night, Patrick saw a vision of a man "whose name was Victoricus, coming as it were from Ireland, with countless letters. And he gave me one of them, and I read the opening words of the letter, which were, 'The voice of the Irish'; and as I read the beginning of the letter I thought that at the same moment I heard their voice — they were those beside the Wood of Voclut, which is near the Western Sea — and thus did they cry out as with one mouth: 'We ask thee, boy, come and walk among us once more.'"

Patrick followed the prophetic call of God and returned to the nation that had enslaved him. He performed many miracles, planted several churches, and led thousands to Christ. He even prophesied of an Irish saint who would follow him by returning the gospel to Britain: "A man-child shall be born of his race, he will be a sage, a prophet, a poet, a beloved lamp, pure, clear, who will utter no falsehood." This prophecy was fulfilled when Saint Columba left Ireland for Scotland.

Key Comment: "Christ be with me, Christ within me, Christ behind me, Christ before me, Christ beside me, Christ to win me; Christ to comfort and restore me; Christ beneath me, Christ above me, Christ in quiet, Christ in danger, Christ in hearts of all that love me, Christ in mouth of friend and stranger."

More: Read Saint Patrick's *Confession* and *Breastplate*.

Sources: Charles W. Colby, *Selections from the Sources of English History, BC 55–AD 1832*, (London: Longmans Green, 1920). Northumbrian Community "Celtic Night Prayer." (Glasgow: Marshall Pickering, 1996).

In such a contentious place, the temptation always is to compromise or become tolerant of other beliefs. Tolerance is the new spirit of the age in our times. The church is being told to compromise its language and beliefs on a wide variety of issues in our culture and society. The church in Pergamum had dropped its guard and was allowing a variety of things to be taught that were harmful to the spiritual growth of its people.

Pergamum is a tough place to start a church and it needs tough people who stand up for the things of God, even if their stand leads to death, as in the case of Antipas. The call to repentance is a reminder that the call on them as a church is to stand up and fight. This is a corrective word that enables the church to regroup and recover their initial calling.

There is a protocol necessary in the church for prophetic words of this type. We will deal with this much more thoroughly in the second journal of this series, which is Prophetic Protocol.

PROPHECY CAN PROVIDE DIRECTION
AND ENHANCE VISION

Direction, purpose, and vision are vital for individuals and groups. Where there is no vision, the people perish. From within a church, a prophetic word can be released that will provide a focus for our goals and plans. Personal and corporate vision can be birthed with a depth of faith. It is vital we understand and have confidence in the Lord's call upon our lives.

CONFIRMATION IS A VITAL PART OF PROPHECY

We may need to be cautious where there has been a great deal of internal prophecy bringing direction and envisioning. All words need to be tested, especially those that pertain to the direction of a church. To avoid error or deception, it is a good idea to ask an established, mature prophetic ministry, unattached to the particular church, to give some confirmation from the outside. This person has no ax to grind and no flag to wave, therefore they can be impartial and objective, both in the judging process and in bringing a confirming word.

Words of direction and vision that come into the church from the outside can have a transforming effect on the work. Just as a word blessing the hidden treasure in an individual can bring that gift to the surface, so too can a word ignite a body. I have lost count of the times when God has used me in this manner. All over the world, I have been given the great opportunity to speak prophetically to churches. In many cases I have confirmed ideas, concepts, and dreams that have been part of the conversation and prayers of leadership teams as they have deliberated on the next stage of their vision and calling.

On one particularly memorable occasion, I prophesied a conversation between two elders that had taken place while they were riding to the very meeting I was speaking at. They had been surprised to discover that they both had the same idea about creating a new pastoral initiative. During that meeting, I called them both out and laid hands on them for a new pastoral anointing. It was a God-given confirmation.

Prophecy can provide dynamic insight into situations not made clear by Scripture. It provides a distinctive perception of the things of God that may not be gained from the counsel of the Bible. Scripture provides an overall picture of the grand design of God and how to live in the Spirit, but it does not always give us the means or the method to do that effectively. Put simply, the Bible gives strategy while prophecy reveals tactics.

PROPHECY COUNTERS NEGATIVITY

In 2 Chronicles 20, we see a powerful example of the power of prophecy. When some of Judah's greatest enemies aligned against King Jehoshaphat, the people did the one thing they knew to do: they gathered together to seek the Lord for His help. In the face of overwhelming opposition, they prayed.

Jehoshaphat stood before his countrymen and prayed, reminding God of how He had made a covenant with their forefathers. He spoke of the historical accounts of how God had delivered His people again and again. *"For we have no power against this great multitude that is coming against us; nor do we know what to do, but our eyes are upon You,"* Jehoshaphat concluded in verse 12.

Tradition stipulated that they should fast and pray when under attack, but it was the entrance of the prophetic that increased their faith and confidence: *"Then the Spirit of the LORD came upon Jahaziel the son of Zechariah, the son of Benaiah, the son of Jeiel, the son of Mattaniah, a Levite of the sons of Asaph, in the midst of the assembly,"* verse 14 records. Jahaziel prophesied what was to come:

> *...and he said, "Listen, all Judah and the inhabitants of Jerusalem and King Jehoshaphat: thus says the Lord to you, 'Do not fear or be dismayed because of this great multitude, for the battle is not yours but God's. 'Tomorrow go down against them. Behold, they will come up by the ascent of Ziz, and you will find them at the end of the valley in front of the wilderness of Jeruel. 'You need not fight in this battle; station yourselves, stand and see the salvation of the Lord on your behalf, O Judah and Jerusalem.' Do not fear or be dismayed; tomorrow go out to face them, for the Lord is with you."* (2 Chronicles 20:15–17)

Prophecy made them tactically aware of God's plan for the situation. It was prophecy that pinpointed the exact whereabouts of the enemy and showed Judah how to fight and what to expect. The entrance of the prophetic birthed confidence: *"Then the Levites of the children of the Kohathites and of the children of the Korahites stood up to praise the LORD God of Israel with voices loud and high"* (2 Chronicles 20:19). We need to live by every word that comes from the mouth of God, ordering our lives by Scripture and being led by the Holy Spirit. To be sons and daughters of God, we must earnestly desire to move in prophecy.

Prophecy is also vital in spiritual warfare. *"This charge I commit to you, son Timothy, according to the prophecies previously made concerning you, that by them you may wage the good warfare,"* Paul wrote in 1 Timothy 1:18. We need to use prophecies to fight the enemy and the circumstances of life.

Just as Jehoshaphat defeated the enemy on the basis of the prophetic word given to him, so we too can harness the power of the prophetic and defeat our spiritual enemies. Judah had been so energized by Jahaziel's word that it broke camp singing. We must never underestimate the power of the prophetic.

Joshua followed a similar pattern of listening and responding to a prophetic word in Joshua 6:1–5:

PROPHECY INCREASES FAITH

Now Jericho was tightly shut because of the sons of Israel; no one went out and no one came in. The Lord said to Joshua, "See, I have given Jericho into your hand, with its king and the valiant warriors. "You shall march around the city, all the men of war circling the city once. You shall do so for six days. "Also seven priests shall carry seven trumpets of rams' horns before the ark; then on the seventh day you shall march around the city seven times, and the priests shall blow the trumpets. "It shall be that when they make a long blast with the ram's horn, and when you hear the sound of the trumpet, all the people shall shout with a great shout; and the wall of the city will fall down flat, and the people will go up every man straight ahead."

Jericho fell exactly as Joshua had been told it would. The method of Jehoshaphat and Joshua should never have worked; you won't find them in any kind of war manual as a way to win a battle. Great generals don't mimic their strategy. No record exists of other armies being destroyed by singing, nor a fortified city falling to marching feet and shouting voices. But in God's realm, prophecy and warfare go together.

PROPHECY OPENS THE TEACHING OF THE WORD AND CONFIRMS PREACHING

In 1 Corinthians 13:2, the apostle Paul wrote, *"And though I have the gift of prophecy, and understand all mysteries and all knowledge."* In biblical language, a mystery is a secret, hidden thought concealed by God from humanity for a period of time. Several times in my life, the Lord has given me a flash of revelation that has driven me to search Scripture and opened up new areas of truth for me. Until that revelatory insight, those things had been hidden from me. The revelation inspired fresh study into the Scriptures.

It is sad when people get the flash of insight but don't follow it through. This can cause heresy and error rather than birthing deep revelatory truth. They present a portion of truth and a lot of speculation.

SAINT BRIGID

Lived: 450 to 523

Prophetic Synopsis: Renowned for her generosity and hospitality, this Irish saint was also wonderfully prophetic. In a prophecy eerily similar to one given by her contemporary, Saint Patrick, she foretold the ministry of Saint Columba, even giving the saint's Irish name and mother's identity: "The man-child of long-sided Ethne, as a sage he is a-blossoming. Columcille, pure without blemish. It is not oversoon to perceive him."

As a child, Brigid was taken by the Holy Spirit to Bethlehem. It was an experience that changed her life.

When she was young, she would give her father's personal belongings and food to the poor. No matter how many times her father told her not to, she would give away clothing, pottery, and food to anyone who needed it more than she did. Her father became so frustrated that he decided to sell her to a king. He left her at the castle gate while he went in and discussed a price. Meanwhile, out at the gate, Brigid was approached by beggar, asking for money. She gave the poor man her father's sword. Her dad and the king were amazed. The king wouldn't buy her, saying, "She is too good for me — I could never win her obedience."

In an age when women had little authority, God gave Brigid hers. When the time came for Brigid to become a nun, she and a group of women asked Bishop Mel to bless them. Brigid was silent out of humility and respect before the great leader. But as the Bishop prayed, he saw the Spirit of God descend on her. He called her out: "I have no power in this matter," the Bishop said. "God has ordained Brigid."

Key Comment: "May God our Father, our strength and light, bless you beyond even all you would ask. For the weather is always right for the sowing of good seed."

More: Read *Brigid's Cloak* by Bryce Milligan and Helen Cann or *The Celtic Saints* by Nigel Pennick.

Sources: Bryce Milligan, *Birgid's Cloak: An Ancient Irish Story* (Grand Rapids, MI: Eerdmans Books for Young Readers, 2002). Nigel Pennick, *The Celtic Saints: An Illustrated and Authoritative Guide to These Extraordinary Men and Women* (Sterling Pub Co Inc, 1997).

They inadvertently corrupt the word with their own ideas and concepts that, if left unchecked, can cause real damage. Continuous revelation leads to study and prayer.

As the flow of revelation has increased in my life, I have scaled back my scheduled commitments. I want to have the time necessary to study, meditate, and pray as part of my response to the words given to me. I currently spend four months each year in meditation.

The apostle Paul understood the power of revelation in unwrapping the mysteries of the kingdom of God. *"By revelation He made known to me the mystery ... which in other ages was not made known to the sons of men, as it has now been revealed by the Spirit to His holy apostles and prophets,"* he wrote in Ephesians 3:3–5. Passages like this highlight the need for prophets to promote and provoke active judging and weighing of all prophetic utterances. By opening up the Word, we can wander into the danger of having false doctrine being added to the hazard of false prophecy. We must relentlessly seek God on issues like these.

Prophecy by itself will not save us from ignorance, nor will it solve all of our problems. The Corinthian church had a well-established prophetic presence but still struggled with sin, immorality, and carnality. As Paul told them in 1 Corinthians 13:9, *"For we know in part and we prophesy in part."* Our prophecy can be incomplete, and we must remember that.

THERE IS NO BREAKTHROUGH WITHOUT FOLLOW-THROUGH

Prophecy can also confirm the preaching of the Word, both before and after teaching. It is common in many churches to see a word given during worship tie in perfectly with the sermon to come.

As good Bereans we love to search the scriptures to see if these things are true. Prophetic input will drive us to the Bible not as Pharisees to disprove something (because they already hold a mindset, they have no intention of changing) but to look for confirmation and connection. Prophecy is a *complement* to scripture, not an addition.

PROPHECY CAN RELEASE THE CHURCH INTO NEW DOCTRINE OR PRACTICES

The gift of prophecy also has a future aspect to it—a "now, but not yet" paradoxical feel to it. The book of Revelation is a perfect example of this; it is entirely predictive and prophetic, forth telling and foretelling.

When I write that prophecy can release a church into a new doctrine, I want to make it clear that we are not talking about new doctrines or practices never before heard of in the universal Church. Rather, I am speaking of a doctrine that might be completely new to a particular body of people.

Several years ago, the Lord gave me a series of prophetic words for certain churches concerning the type of people God would give them in five years' time. One church in particular was primarily Caucasian and very wealthy; the Lord told me that He was about to send them people who were broken, used, downtrodden, abused, abusers, addicts, alcoholics, involved in the occult, single parents, fatherless, and outcast.

PROPHECY CAN OPEN US UP TO NEW EXPERIENCES OF GOD

To their eternal credit, the church came back several weeks later asking for help. They fully understood that the arrival of these people would totally change the face of their church. The repercussions of the word were astounding. They knew they had been given time to make changes, and they wanted to be ready.

With a prophetic promise of harvest on the horizon, we knew the enemy would increase its attack on the church. To help them survive the storm, we taught the church about defensive spiritual warfare. This was a concept they had never considered before. They learned how to keep their own homes and lives free from spiritual attack and how to fight off sickness and financial need. For many of these people, this was new ground; it was a revelation of a new truth and a new practice.

Later on, we taught them offensive warfare in life, prayer, and worship. We became more militant in our outlook. In worship, the church praised Jesus as the warrior King. After that, we taught about having a Joshua mindset; they became people who spoiled for a fight. They became people who could move into new territories promised by God, expecting a fight and expecting to win.

After the calling comes the training. A similar pattern unfolded in Acts 10, when Peter led Cornelius and his Gentile household to Christ. When God called Peter to go, he did. His prophetic vision on the rooftop the day before prepared him for a new call. Peter was given the same prophetic vision on three occasions. The interpretation of which called Peter to break with a centuries-old tradition and open up a way for Gentile people to know the Lord. In that day and time this was scary stuff, small wonder that Peter was perplexed and had misgivings!

Indeed, it was only when he actually crossed the Gentile threshold of the house of Cornelius that revelation dawned on him. *"In truth I perceive that God shows no partiality,"* Peter said in Acts 10:34–35. *"But in every nation whoever fears Him and works righteousness is accepted by Him."* This lifted the early Church out of its Jewish context and made the salvation of Christ available to the whole world. It released men like Paul, Luke, Barnabas, Silas, John Mark, and Philip to preach the gospel to all nations. A new doctrine had been released through Peter's prophetic vision and his willingness to follow Christ's commands.

PROPHECY PROVIDES INSIGHT INTO COUNSELING SITUATIONS

Counseling is a vital ministry in the Church today; it has become a necessary part of working out our salvation before God. However, the Church has done a great disservice to many of these people by preaching a poor quality of gospel. Too many believers have received the gospel of "having your needs met in Christ." This has created a generation of people who expect God and, by extension, the Church to do everything for them.

The real gospel, the one preached in Acts, was that Jesus was both Lord and Christ. The apostles' challenge to the unsaved was: "Jesus is Lord; what are you going to do about it?" Two thousand years later, we have developed a Church with an invalid culture, not a warrior mindset.

Counseling should be conducted as part of the introduction to church life and the foundations of a Spirit-filled walk with God. To be most effective, it needs the cooperation of evangelists, pastors, teachers, and prophets—four ministries working together to bring about a good birth and a strong upbringing in the things of God.

PROPHECY INTRODUCES A NEW MINDSET FOR LIFE

The prophetic can get to the heart of a problem in a profound way. *"Even now the ax is laid to the root of the trees,"* Jesus said in Matthew 3:10. *"Therefore every tree which does not bear good fruit is cut down and thrown into the fire."* A prophetic word allows us to focus on Jesus, a paradigm shift that sparks movement and change. Without the supernatural, counseling can focus on problems and processes rather than on Jesus the deliverer.

Prophecy can save a lot of time in counseling sessions. A prophetic word, in season, can save months of work by getting to the basics of an issue. It strips away unhelpful attitudes and layers of deception that people can hide behind. Prophecy, with its attendant associates of words of knowledge and wisdom, can save us from endless hours of dialogue by exposing situations and bringing a quick release. It causes an accelerated breakthrough.

The arrival of the supernatural means we cannot hide behind lies or deception. We can cover nothing up. Understanding this will provoke a level of honesty and godly fear that will break any stranglehold of sin in the lives of believers.

PROPHECY CAN PROVIDE
EVANGELISTIC BREAKTHROUGHS

Paul's call in 1 Corinthians 14:24–25 is something to which every church should aspire:

But if all prophesy, and an unbeliever or an ungifted man enters, he is convicted by all, he is called to account by all; the secrets of his heart are disclosed; and so he will fall on his face and worship God, declaring that God is certainly among you.

Everyone has a dream for their life. The Pharisees were the dream thieves of their day. They stole people's dreams of God, giving them

KING OSWALD

Lived: 605 to 643

Prophetic Synopsis: Oswald, born in Northumbria, the north-eastern corner of England, spent seventeen years on the Isle of Iona learning to be a monk. When his uncle, King Edwin, died, the murderous Cadwallan seized the throne and tormented Oswald's people. So the good prince returned, with his older brother Eanfrid, to rid Northumbria of Cadwallan. But Cadwallan killed Eanfrid almost immediately, leaving Oswald to fend for himself in Northumbria.

Oswald gathered an army of pagan people — men who had never even heard of Jesus Christ. He took his army to a place called Heavenfield to face Cadwallan in one final battle. The night before the battle, Oswald had a dream in which Saint Columba promised him victory. The next morning, Oswald brought together all of his warriors and ordered them to take a knee. He erected a huge wooden cross and bowed his head in prayer, saying, "Let us all kneel and jointly beseech the true and living God Almighty, in His mercy, to defend us from the haughty and fierce enemy, for He knows that we have undertaken a just war for the safety of our nation."

Oswald's army defeated Cadwallan and his much stronger army. Oswald's warriors looked around and decided that there was no earthly way they could have routed Cadwallan so harshly, except for the miraculous intervention of Oswald's God. His dream and prayer opened the people's hearts and made them hungry for this newfound Savior. Oswald sent for help from Iona and received it in the form of Saint Aidan.

Key Comment: "Why should these fast while I am feasting? God loves all alike, and not less the poor, but rather more."

More: Read *The Ecclesiastical History of the English People* by Bede.

Sources: Bede, *The Eccleciasticaly History of the English People; The Greater Chronicle; Bede's Lettter to Egbert,* eds Judith McClure and Roger Collins (Oxford; New York: Oxford University Press, 1994).

instead a sterile atmosphere filled with rules rather than an encounter with a loving God who understood their aspirations.

Many times the Lord has enabled me to see the dream of an indi-

PROPHECY PRODUCES A GREATER AWARENESS OF GOD'S NATURE

vidual and to relate it to them in joyful humility. In every case there has been an astonishment and delight (and not a few tears!) as people have understood for the first time who they are in themselves. To be known by God when you are not fully aware of your own identity is a powerful moment that provokes worship in all manner of people.

It is amazing to see what can happen when a pre-Christian witnesses dynamic, dramatic, and accurate words of prophecy. They are always strongly affected by such obvious ministry of the Holy Spirit. For many, this is their first real introduction to the Lord and they fall in love with the God of dreams and want to follow Him.

I have seen many atheists and agnostics come to Christ through the gift of prophecy. This should come as no surprise; after all, Jesus Himself outlined the Holy Spirit's role in John 16:8–11:

And He, when He comes, will convict the world concerning sin and righteousness and judgment; concerning sin, because they do not believe in Me; and concerning righteousness, because I go to the Father and you no longer see Me; and concerning judgment, because the ruler of this world has been judged.

Prophecy, by uncovering past needs and issues, can provide an agenda for repentance, restitution, and revival.

Prophetic evangelism is a growing phenomenon in the Church today. It causes the supernatural power of God to break through into people's lives. A number of churches around the world are going door to door in their communities and working by words of knowledge and prophecy. God knows which homes are ready for sowing and ripe for reaping. Gaining God's perspective provides a prayer agenda that will enable us to go to certain houses with something specific to say.

PROPHECY PROVIDES AN AGENDA FOR PRAYER

Prayer, in its purest form, is finding out what God wants to do and then asking Him to do it. *"And whatever things you ask in prayer, believing, you will receive,"* Jesus said in Matthew 21:22. Why, then, do we seemingly receive so few answers to prayer today? Prayer, as it is taught today in most churches, is sporadic in its effect. Most of us have been brought up in a tradition that when something bad happens, prayer must begin immediately. This seems reasonable and even righteous, but on a deeper level, it actually hinders the power of God to work on our behalf. In my experience in churches and friendships, I have seen that when we pray too soon, we usually pray in unbelief. We find ourselves praying out of the shock or trauma of the situation itself, and we pray out of our panic, our worry, our anxiety, and our concern.

We enter God's presence with thanksgiving and His courts with praise. Rejoicing as a lifestyle enables us to live doubt free in our faith. It maintains a closeness of connection to the Father so that faith, peace, and joy are operating on a high level continuously.

A joyful heart finds it easy to trust and to hear the voice of God. We can come before the Lord in worshipful listening in order to hear what His heart is for us in this situation.

Jesus is praying for us. The Holy Spirit is praying for us. We are the third part of a threefold cord in prayer. That means we must pray *with* the answer—not to try to find one.[2]

By asking God for a revelation of His will for a situation, we change the atmosphere of our prayer. When God tells us the way something will unfold, we can't help but pray full of faith and confidence! This is why most successful prayer initiatives have their roots in the prophetic.

In 1982, God began to show me things He wanted to do in the British church. I saw that the Charity Commission would be given real teeth to expose financial malpractice and to comment on value-for-money in all voluntary agencies, including churches. In the two decades since, we have seen the charitable status of several agencies revoked. I also saw that the government would invest millions of pounds in community endeavors. After doing a major value-for-money study, some long-established charities folded, while new ones were created. The Church had the opportunity to step into that vacuum and create real social change.

Some churches did just that. I think of my hometown of Manchester, England, where a group of churches got together and envisioned a long-term plan for the city. To get the ball rolling, they decided to start saving some money. It took them a few years, but finally they had enough money in the bank to put their plan in motion.

2 The practice of this type of prayer is found in the journal on "Crafted Prayer," part of the Being with God series (www.brilliantbookhouse.com).

Together, the churches approached Manchester's civic government, police department, social services, and business community with an idea called Eden 2000. With the help of the city's experts, they picked the worst neighborhood in Manchester. This particular area was full of crime. The streets were filthy. It had been compared by the media to a war zone. It was a godless, hopeless place.

But the churches were up to the challenge. Together, they mobilized 20,000 Christians over several weeks. These Christians went into the neighborhood and started working. They painted houses—many hundreds. They cleaned up gardens. They picked up trash. They planted roses. They built playgrounds. They prayed for everyone they met. They started two churches. They worked and worked and worked. In those two weeks, not a single crime was committed in the area. At the end of Eden 2000, people were weeping. "Don't leave us!" they cried. The neighborhood has been a changed place ever since.

PROPHECY RELEASES US TO EXPLORE THE FUTURE AND TO OWN THE PRESENT

In 1982, God also showed me that a network of deliverance and intercessory ministries would bloom across the nation. These works provide a strategy for warfare and inter-church (and inter-city) prayer links. They share information, training and equipping programs, and a common warfare strategy. The overwhelming success of the 24–7 Prayer movement is just one highly visible component of the fulfillment of this word.

A word about unity was also given to me. I used to think the name "United Kingdom" was a joke. However, God has shown me it is a prophetic name. The Lord is raising up champions in the Celtic nations—men and women who have a tremendous anointing for unity. They will turn the hearts of the nations toward one another.

We will have conferences and conventions aimed at more than just unity—they will actively promote reconciliation, apology, and restoration. Forgiveness and healing will flow as the north-south divide in England dies. Inter-country and inter-city rivalry will perish. Lancashire will stop fighting the War of the Roses with Yorkshire. Cities—even Manchester and Liverpool—will be joined in heart and spirit. Strongholds of history, bigotry, treachery, and betrayal will be torn down. As these things are finally dealt with, we will see economic and spiritual revival break out in these areas.

The Holy Spirit came to Jesus' followers when *"they were all with one accord in one place"* (Acts 2:1). The Spirit finds unity irresistible. Conversely, the demonic inhabits disunity. Unity can start with one person making a stand for love. What we need is active personal, individual, and corporate promoting of unity in every church, home, and city in every nation. The Eden 2000 project in Manchester is a prophetic template of what God can accomplish when believers unite.

Finally, God showed me that there was a quickening spirit upon the British Church, particularly on established institutional Christianity. I have spent thousands of hours working with domestic churches in various denominations, thoroughly enjoying the relationships I have built there. These groups offer a fascinating mix of growth, change, passion for Jesus, and a new radicalism about church planting and community involvement. They exhibit a great hunger for reality and the supernatural presence of God.

SAINT AUGUSTINE OF HIPPO

Lived: 354 to 430

Prophetic Synopsis: Few have done more to shape Christian theology and thought than St. Augustine. Born to a pagan father and devoutly Christian mother, Augustine struggled through-out his early life to find the one true path. The wilder he lived, the less contentment he found.

His mother, Monica, prayed diligently for her son's salvation. In answer to her prayers, God gave her a stunningly prophetic dream. In it, a Man of Light asked her why she was so sad. "When she replied that her tears were for the soul I had lost, he told her to take heart for, if she looked carefully, she would see that where she was, there also was I," Augustine wrote in his *Confessions*. "And when she looked, she saw me standing beside her on the same rule."

Nine years later, her dream would come true when Augustine met the Light for himself. "What I saw was something quite, quite different from any light we know on earth," Augustine said. "I realized that I was far away from You. It was as though I were in a land where all is different from Your own and I heard Your voice calling from on high, saying, 'I am the food of full-grown men. Grow and you shall feed on Me. But you shall not change Me into your own substance, as you do with the food of your body. Instead you shall be changed into Me.' And, far off, I heard Your voice saying, 'I am the God who is.' I heard Your voice, as we hear voices that speak to our hearts, and at once, I had no cause to doubt."

Key Comment: "Faith is to believe what you do not see; the reward of this faith is to see what you believe."

More: Read Saint Augustine's *Confessions and City of God.*

Sources: St. Augustine of Hippo, *Confessions,* ed. John Rotelle, trans. R. S. Pine-Coffin (New York: Penguin, 1961). Saint Augustine, *The City of God,* trans. Marcus D. D. Dods (New York: The Modern Library, 1950).

The British Church is more influential in the Western church world now than it has been in centuries. What we thought might take years to accomplish has taken months, thanks to God's grace.

Each of these prophetic words provided me with an agenda to pray. I have spent countless hours and days praying into these things. In prophecy, God's will is expressed. Where God's will is made known, we have the basis for an ongoing prayer thrust until His will comes to pass.

FOUR COMMON ARGUMENTS AGAINST PROPHECY

While prophecy seems to have come to the forefront of progressive church life in recent years, the truth is that it has been an integral and vibrant part of Christianity throughout the ages. It is a rich part of the heritage of God's people. The Bible makes it clear that Jesus Christ is our Prophet, Priest, and King. Sadly, much of the Church does very little study of the verses that clearly portray Christ as prophet:

And the crowds were saying, "This is the prophet Jesus, from Nazareth in Galilee. (Matthew 21:11)

Therefore when the people saw the sign which He had performed, they said, "This is truly the Prophet who is to come into the world. (John 6:14)

And He said to them, "What things?" And they said to Him, "The things about Jesus the Nazarene, who was a prophet mighty in deed and word in the sight of God and all the people." (Luke 24:19)

DOES THE BIBLE REPLACE SPIRITUAL GIFTS?

Essentially, dispensationalists argue that because we have the whole revelation of God in Scripture, the gifts of the Holy Spirit are no longer necessary. Of course, many of the people who hold this view still pray for a miracle or healing when a loved one is sick! Prophecy is done away with, they argue, because the perfect — the Scripture — has come, using an interpretation of 1 Corinthians 13:8–10 as their foundation: *"Love never fails. But whether there are prophecies, they will fail; whether there are tongues, they will cease; whether there is knowledge, it will vanish away. For we know in part and we prophesy in part. But when that which is perfect has come, then that which is in part will be done away."*

Yet this argument falls down when the same perfect Word of God, less than a chapter later, encourages the Church to *"pursue love, and desire spiritual gifts, but especially that you may prophesy"* (1 Corinthians 14:1).

Dispensationalism has been rightly discredited in a large part of the Christian Church because it conflicts with a number of things Jesus said concerning the Person and work of the Holy Spirit in John 14–16:

...PROMOTE UNBELIEF IN THE NATURAL WORLD

Truly, truly, I say to you, he who believes in Me, the works that I do, he will do also; and greater works than these he will do; because I go to the Father. (John 14:12)

But the Helper, the Holy Spirit, whom the Father will send in My name, He will teach you all things, and bring to your remembrance all things that I said to you. (John 14:26)

If you abide in Me, and My words abide in you, ask whatever you wish, and it will be done for you. (John 15:7)

When the Helper comes, whom I will send to you from the Father, that is the Spirit of truth who proceeds from the Father, He will testify about Me. (John 15:26)

And He, when He comes, will convict the world concerning sin and righteousness and judgment: concerning sin, because they do not believe in Me; and concerning righteousness, because I go to the Father and you no longer see Me; and concerning judgment, because the ruler of this world has been judged. (John 16:8–11)

But when He, the Spirit of truth, comes, He will guide you into all the truth; for He will not speak on His own initiative, but whatever He hears, He will speak; and He will disclose to you what is to come. (John 16:13)

All things that the Father has are Mine; therefore I said that He takes of Mine and will disclose it to you. (John 16:15)

The doctrine of dispensationalism completely conflicts with Jesus' own teaching of the purpose of His death, burial, resurrection, and ascension — the four most important moments in the spiritual history of the world. Jesus Himself taught that the Holy Spirit was to have a key place in the ongoing life of a Christian. Dispensationalism clashes with the Gospels like a loud cymbal being fiercely played in an otherwise perfectly orchestrated symphony. It is a confusing, offensive, and disturbing hypothesis that does not align with the Bible.

The true meaning of 1 Corinthians 13:12 simply refers to the end of all things and a full revelation of God to each believer. For now, we see dimly in comparison with that face-to-face, eternal revelation to come. In heaven, we will fully know — and be fully known. This verse is clearly not talking about this life but the eternal life to come. In that place, prophecy will not be needed: absolute perfection and communion with God will reign. I can hardly wait for that time!

The idea of dispensationalism is an insult to the person and sacrifice of Jesus. In all of His teaching on the Holy Spirit, He never once mentioned that the gifts were temporary or that they would run out before His return. In fact, the Holy Spirit, and His gifts and graces, are a permanent fixture in the Church to enable the bride of Christ to be made ready and presentable for her Bridegroom. The Spirit empowers us to preach the gospel, with signs and wonders following, to the very ends of the earth. There is so much work to do; we need the Holy Spirit now more than ever. Why would God withhold the Spirit from every generation, except one, when He has given us so much to accomplish?

Dispensationalists believe that around the time the final early Church apostle died, the gifts of the Holy Spirit evaporated. If this is true, why is there no mention of it in early Christian writings? Surely the whole of Christendom would have been brokenhearted that the heavens suddenly turned to brass. How did it happen? When did it happen? Was it immediate? Was it the instant the apostle John died? If someone had prayed at 11:55 a.m. for a healing, would it have happened? If that same person prayed six minutes later, after the gifts were taken, would they have missed their chance? It just seems so ludicrous to forget healing, wholeness, and fullness—heaven is now closed! You're on your own, folks. One moment healing is a sign of God's power and the expression of His heart to the world; the next it's gone.

At Pentecost, the apostle Peter spoke these words (Acts 2:38–39):

Peter said to them, "Repent, and each of you be baptized in the name of Jesus Christ for the forgiveness of your sins; and you will receive the gift of the Holy Spirit.

"For the promise is for you and your children and for all who are far off, as many as the Lord our God will call to Himself."

It's hard to get further off than two thousand years later, but Peter's promise still rings through the ages and includes us.

Peter's prophetic word was given in a moment when the Holy Spirit was being poured out. Tongues and interpretation were commanding the attention of those who did not believe. Healings were about to become everyday occurrences for believers. It was made in the context of the supernatural invading the earth, causing an explosion of understanding and desire for God. The Holy Spirit turned that city upside down and inside out. This revolution had massive repercussions around the world.

THE KINGDOM OF HEAVEN IS A SHOW-AND-TELL REALM OF POWER AND MIRACLES

Into that context, Peter spoke prophetically to those early, and largely unsaved, people gathered to witness a miracle. He stood and taught them from history, weaving in the truth of Jesus for the present day and prophesying of the future.

The gifts of the Holy Spirit are indeed for today; to believe otherwise is to believe deception.

DOES PREOCCUPATION WITH THE GIFTS PREVENT EFFECTIVE EVANGELISM?

Adherents to this idea teach that one needs to strip themselves of anything that would divert them from the primary objective of preaching the gospel. It cannot be denied that some churches and small groups have become self-indulgent "bless me" clubs where the gifts are practiced endlessly on other believers. This breeds a type of "spiritual junkie," an addict looking for another hit of prayer. Many people chase that experiential relationship with the Holy Spirit for the purpose of self-gratification and excitement. They bounce from church to church, looking for the next "move of God." Much of this adolescent spiritual behavior is due to the fact that many Christians have a poor understanding of the kingdom of God.

There are three aspects to establishing the kingdom of God on Earth in a post-modern world. They are renewal, revival, and reformation.

First and foremost, we are lovers of God. It is our primary goal to live by the first commandment: "love the Lord your God with *all* your heart, soul, mind, and strength." The present-day church needs a renewal of her first-love experience. We must value intimacy and have a vision for it as part of individual and corporate life. We must prize worship and take steps to improve and increase our worship on every level. We must disciple people into a continuous joyful encounter with the living God. We need to teach them how to praise the Lord, practice continuous thanksgiving, and to embrace the joy of rejoicing as a lifestyle.

Revival is not about the lost getting saved. One cannot revive something that has never been alive. Revival is therefore about the church returning to a place of passion for the world in which we live and the lost in particular. Revival is about the restoration of passion for that which Jesus died to save. Revival occurs when the church joyfully takes up the ministry of reconciliation and becomes ambassadors for heaven. The Great Commission and the Second Commandment are one and the same.

THE GOSPEL IS NOT JUST IN WORD BUT IN POWER!

When the church lives fully in the first and second commandments, then we are moving fully in renewal and revival in the Spirit. The two when combined will force the world to experience a reformation. The walls of the church are knocked flat and what we have as our habitation experience of His presence is suddenly let loose on an unsuspecting world just as it was on the day of Pentecost.

When this occurs we will hear the world crying out today as they did in the early church—the people who have turned the world upside down are here, too! (see Acts 17:6).

We are here to preach the gospel of the kingdom, not just build the Church. The Church comes out of the kingdom — not vice versa. When we understand that we must lay aside everything to seek the kingdom, we will see a renewal occur that will truly honor the Lord.

When we appreciate the fact that everything we know and have must be channeled into establishing the kingdom, we will see church, leadership, lifestyle, pastoring, teaching, and the gifts of the Spirit in a completely different light. When this happens, revival will be upon us.

SAINT CUTHBERT

Lived: 635 to 687

Prophetic Synopsis: Cuthbert was fifteen years old when his life changed forever. While out tending sheep on a hill in Northumbria, he had a vision. As he described it, "Methought I saw a dazzling radiance shine suddenly out of the darkness, and in the midst of the streaming light a choir of angels descended to earth and lo! They were bearing away as in a globe of fire a happy soul." He went to Melrose Abbey and told the monks of his experience. It turns out he had the vision at the exact moment Saint Aidan died. His vision became known as the Passing of Saint Aidan.

Eata, whom Aidan discipled, in turn took Cuthbert and discipled him. Eventually, Cuthbert became the leader of Melrose Abbey. He was very popular throughout Northumbria. "Cuthbert was so skillful a speaker and had such a light in his face and such a love for proclaiming his message that none presumed to hide their inmost secrets, but openly confessed all the wrongdoing for they felt it impossible to conceal their guilt from him," wrote the historian Bede.

Soon, Cuthbert became the spiritual leader of all of Northumbria, taking over at the holy island of Lindisfarne. He loved to be alone with God, to pray and read Scripture.

Cuthbert even prophesied his own death to his best friend, Herebert, who would visit him once a year. Herebert and Cuthbert had a unique relationship: Herebert would spend several hours every day praying for God to help Cuthbert in his leadership duties. Then, once a year, Herebert would visit his friend and Cuthbert would encourage him. One year, Cuthbert told Herebert to ask him for anything because Cuthbert was about to die. Herebert asked him for just one thing: that they would die together. Both died on March 20, 687.

Key Comment: "Christ's soldier is the fittest champion to fight the powers of darkness."

More: Read *The Ecclesiastical History of the English People* by Bede.

Sources: Bede, *The Eccleciastical History of the English People; The Greater Chronicle; Bede's Lettter to Egbert*, eds Judith McClure and Roger Collins (Oxford; New York: Oxford University Press, 1994).

Revival is actually about the Church coming back to her original purpose before God.

This will occur when we allow Jesus to inhabit us. For me, revival can be defined as the Church coming back to a place where God can trust us with the things He really wants to give us. When that happens, there will be a reformation. God will knock down the walls of His Church, and what we have in a Sunday meeting or weekend conference will be the same as what we have in the world. Miracles will happen, God will be in full evidence, people will get saved by the hundreds and thousands, and creation's longing for the sons of God to move in power will be answered.

I believe strongly in prophetic evangelism, words of knowledge for the unsaved, gifts of healing across the whole community, and expressing God's heart prophetically in the earth to all people. This is the gospel I read about in the book of Acts. I have been privileged to see pre-Christians respond to a prophetic word and begin their journey into the kingdom. The supernatural presence of the Holy Spirit, through His graces and gifts, can impact a hard community in a way that simple preaching cannot. The apostle Paul himself said that his preaching was not in word only, but by demonstration of the Holy Spirit.

The truth is that spiritual gifts get people's attention, which makes the Word vibrant and irresistible to them. When I worked in a training company many years ago, I would listen carefully to the things God told me to do. Once, I doubled the value of a contract during a pitch because the Lord told me to. When we won the bid — at a huge profit — my employer's eyes were opened to the power of God. It gave me many opportunities to speak into his life.

It doesn't have to be a million-dollar contract to be God. I have visited strangers' houses and prayed for washing machines to work. What am I, a Maytag repairman? Of course not! I'm just someone who wants God to do miraculous things. "Healing" a washing machine—several times—gave me the opportunity to share my faith with a family that I would have otherwise never met.

I have prophesied many times to pre-Christians and seen some spectacular results as they come to God. One woman had not seen her daughter for four years following a family argument. On a whim, she came to a church where I was preaching. She was shocked when I prophesied over her that not only was her daughter safe but that she would see her in four days and their rift would be healed. No one in that church knew her or her issue—but God did.

PEOPLE LOVE TO SEE GOD AT WORK!

She was astonished when the word came true in the few days following the meeting. "It was like heaven opened and I realized that God knew me but I didn't know Him," she told me afterward. The knowledge that He was interested and concerned about her family drove her to want to know Him for herself.

IS THE FRUIT MORE IMPORTANT THAN THE GIFTS?

In Galatians 5:22–23, the apostle Paul listed the fruit of the Holy Spirit: *"love, joy, peace, longsuffering, kindness, goodness, faithfulness, gentleness, self-control."* It is absolutely true that the Church has many people with supernatural gifting and difficult, shoddy characters. It is also correct to say that there are many nice Christians with no overt manifestation of the power of the Holy Spirit in their lives.

We need both good character, as defined by the fruit, and the power of the Spirit. While it is undoubtedly true that the gifts without the fruit are made worthless (see 1 Corinthians 13:1–2), it is also true that the gospel cannot be preached effectively without power (see Romans 1:16). The word must be confirmed by signs following. People were attracted to Jesus by both His personality and His miracles.

In my schools of prophecy, I have seen many people grow in love because of their training in the gift of prophecy. Their desire for God matures their love for others. They inherit the character-istics of the God whom they want to share with people.

THE FATHER IS RELENTLESSLY KIND

I have said countless times that God is the kindest person I have ever known. Every day, He shows me more of His kind nature. He is full of matchless grace, peace, and rest. His love stretches from everlasting to everlasting. His mercy, patience, and long-suffering are legendary. He is slow to anger and swift to bless, abounding in loving-kindness. Every fruit of the Spirit is in full bloom in His nature. These truths cannot be communicated without affecting the giver as well as the word's receiver.

The fruit is not more important than the gift. We must not let the enemy push us into a choice that the Holy Spirit has not asked us to make. In matters of morality, the fruit of our characters must always take precedence. In times of development, fruit and gift grow together. Fruit does not grow well in a vacuum. We want the fullness of God—both gift and fruit.

ARE THE GIFTS OF THE SPIRIT DANGEROUS?

Are the gifts of the Spirit dangerous? I certainly hope so! They should be dangerous to the world, hazardous to the health of the enemy, and a threat to our apathy and indifference. Prophecy is attacking, stimulating, and provoking. It is designed to put a sharp edge on our relationship with God in how we live our lives and handle truth.

The Bible itself says truth is dangerous. *"For the word of God is living and active and sharper than any two-edged sword, and piercing as far as the division of soul and spirit, of both joints and marrow, and able to judge the thoughts and intentions of the heart,"* says Hebrews 4:12. It can cut both ways and needs careful handling. We would never stop using Scripture, even if it cut us to the quick—why then fear the cut of prophecy?

We can no longer afford to ignore things because they are dangerous. Apathy is the most dangerous attitude in the Church, but there are entire communities who have not managed to avoid it. Unbelief is like a dangerous cancer to the things of God, but millions of people are affected by it. No one would ever suggest that we cease preaching or teaching in case we fell into error. Instead, we must work together in defense of truth and the proclamation of the Word of God. In prophecy, we must teach people how to be in the Spirit when they speak. Whether we prophesy, preach, or teach, the same principle applies: there is safety in the anointing of God.

TRUTH: THE BEST SAFEGUARD

In the Church today, we are seeing a resurgence of the prophetic gift and ministry. Unfortunately, with the true comes the counterfeit. Abuse, misuse, and deception will abound along with the correct use of prophecy. Clearly, we need to know how to handle the gift, ministry, and impact within the work of God.

Throughout Church history, there has been false prophecy and false teaching. If we look objectively at the past two millennia, we find that many more churches have been ruined by false teaching than by false prophecy. For example, teaching on accountability in the 1970s led many leaders into heavy shepherding and accusations of control and domination. Accountability is right and proper, but only if it is God-centered — not man-centered. The truth of proper biblical accountability has been marred by the practice that was taught and encouraged. Should we now abandon this truth for fear of further misuse or abuse? Or should we seek to introduce proper use of accountable behavior as an honor to God?

Where there has been abuse, we must work even harder to reclaim the truth. The alternative is to have dozens of "no-go" areas in our churches and to lose massive parts of the gospel.

Many people's lives have been damaged by wrong pastoral advice — far more than the prophetic. Hardly any checks and balances exist for the role of a pastor. It seems pastors can get away with almost

THE WHEAT ALWAYS GROWS UP WITH THE WEEDS

anything. There are even some pastors who will not allow themselves to be challenged without an explosion of some sort happening. Yet no one has proposed the need to dismantle the pastoral ministry.

One of the major problems in the Church today is the number of people who are inadequately birthed into the kingdom of God. Salvation is more a process than it is an instantaneous event. Many people's lives are touched by the Holy Spirit and are brought into a measure of real change. However, if this is not followed up with good teaching, pastoring, and discipling, people's lives will not be fully claimed for the gospel.

Poor evangelism and preaching have created a back-door Christianity, in which people come to Christ on the basis of having their needs met rather than the demand to submit to His lordship. In spite of this, when people talk about balance and accountability, they are inevitably connected with prophetic ministry. It is true that a prophet on his own is out of balance—but then, a pastor, teacher, or evangelist on his own is also out of balance.

This factor has caused more widespread damage in the Church of Jesus Christ than any loose prophetic cannon. The only answer to misuse in all areas of Church life is not non-use but proper use. Truth is always our best safeguard against deviation.

Spiritual leaders must not discourage gifting on the basis that it could be wrong or dangerous. We must use every opportunity to exercise our people in rightly hearing the word of truth. Sadly, many leaders are more concerned with avoiding conflict and difficulty than prospering from those words.

It is far easier to create suspicion and fear in people's minds than to tackle the issues involved. Allowing these things grieves the Holy Spirit, however, and our only response must be to apologize, repent, and change our ways.

Since the earliest Bible times, there has been false prophecy. Why should we be surprised by it today? Why don't we accept that the existence of a counterfeit only further proves the existence of the authentic?

OUR RESPONSE

Our hearts must be filled with a desire for God's truth. This hunger needs to consume everything within us. Integrity is created when we are prepared to break through every barrier, cost, and issue in order to be what is right and proper. We need to *be* the truth, not just *know* it. The truth that prophecy is for today must be appropriated by the whole Church. Part of that ownership is a determination to work through all of the anomalies and dilemmas of releasing the prophetic gift and ministry properly.

The Church is pregnant with the prophetic. Care is needed to bring that prophetic seed to full term. The labor pains are yet to come for the whole ministry; the joy of birthing a new prophetic environment throughout the whole body of Christ will be worth all of the suffering we must endure.

Jesus said, "My sheep know my voice." The heart of the issue is not just about a spiritual gift. It is concerning our relationship with the Lord. We cannot build a relationship with someone if we cannot hear what they are saying. If a Christian chooses to believe that God no longer speaks to His people, then they had better get as close as possible to God so that they can lip read!

This boils down into a quest for true spiritual maturity. God's goal is to see His children walk as fully mature sons and daughters — believers who can be trusted completely.

The Lord has sent His Spirit into our hearts whereby we cry, "Abba, Father" (Galatians 4:6). This is a relational paradox.

A paradox is two opposing ideas contained in the same truth. God is a father and also a judge. He is full of mercy and also justice. He has compassion and also moves in judgment.

We have two types of relationship with the Lord. First, we learn to live before Him as a much loved child. We practice a childlike faith and innocence. We learn to simply relax and trust in His greatness. When under utmost pressure, we know we can lift our arms up and expect His greatness to overwhelm us and lift us up into a higher place. Children are uncomplicated, simple, and trusting.

CHILDLIKE TRUST IS THE BEDROCK OF MATURE FAITH

Second, we learn to say "father" as an adult in the Spirit, to speak out of a place of growing maturity in who the Lord is making us to be. "For as many as are led by the Spirit of God, these are the sons of God" (Romans 8:14). A significant difference exists between being a child of God and being a son of God. We are all children of God, but not all of us, yet, are sons (daughters) of God.

The difference between the two is "learned" experience. As we grow in Christ we experience the other side of the relational paradox. We learn how to move from a different place of relational anointing. We do not outgrow the childlike stage so as to discard it. Rather we move across the range of relational power from Abba to Father. We need both. The childlike faith and trust in the bigness of God are hugely important to maintain as we move out in the Spirit and encounter the wide variety of problems, issues, and crises that life will present. It is the bedrock of our relationship with the majesty of God.

The adult son is just as necessary and vital to the increase of the kingdom. We are mature men and women who can move out in the faith, power, and authority that we have allowed the Holy Spirit to develop in our relationship with the Father in Jesus. It is so wonderful to be in Christ Jesus, praying to the Father by the power of the Holy Spirit.

Every time we encounter a new level of anointing and warfare, we do so as a much loved child. We explore this new realm with childlike trust and wide-eyed wonder. We appropriate it with the grace and simplicity of a childlike relationship. Then the Holy Spirit teaches us to move out in presence, authority, and power into a place of dynamic faith as a mature person in our experience of God. It is most delightful for us to have that range of relational experience to develop in the course of life with all its attendant issues and difficulties.

As a child before the Father, we revel in His bigness. We are in awe of His majesty and His capability. He really can do anything! We are amazed at His capacity for us, His willing heart toward us. We revel in His intentionality and promise. We trust Him implicitly; He is our Daddy.

As an adult before the Father, we revel in His authority, passion, vision, and faith. We love to stand in the problem, holding on to the promise, knowing that the provision will come to us. We love His values and principles. We treat them as our own.

As a child, we are trusting the Lord. As an adult son, we are learning to be trusted by Him. Our goal is to get to the place where our maturity is a source of great delight to the Father. "This is My beloved Son, in whom I am well pleased" (Matthew 3:17). That moment signified a huge upgrade for Jesus, from carpenter's son into His supernatural call to be the Messiah. Fully mature sons and daughters receive an anointing that they have never walked in before. They know by experience how to be available to the purposes of God and constantly wait on and attend to Him. They are consistent in their service to Him. Developing spiritual maturity is the call of every Christian—and every prophetic voice.

THE OBJECTIVE OF PROPHECY

REFLECTIONS, EXERCISES, AND ASSIGNMENTS

The following exercises are designed with this particular chapter in mind. Please work through them carefully before going on to the next chapter. Take time to reflect on your life journey as well as your prophetic development. Learn to work well with the Holy Spirit and people whom God has put around you so that you will grow in grace, humility, and wisdom in the ways of God.

Graham

WHAT CONSTITUTES MATURITY?

We live in a show-and-tell world. People want to see something, not just hear something. We have a magnificent opportunity to develop a supernatural presence in the Holy Spirit.

In this context we need prophecy that is capable of an expression from heaven whilst being rooted in the parameters of Scripture. It is so important that this vital gift is not left merely in the hands of the idle, the unprepared, and those without a sense of purpose.

Maturity is earned in this context by the following:

- Develop a relationship between your love of Scripture and your use of the gift. All prophecy in the Bible is planned, developed, prepared, rehearsed, and clearly thought through. What must change in your style of delivery, content, and preparation of prophecy in order to conform to a biblical base and preparation?

- Prophecy provides much needed insights, perspectives, and wisdom in order to enable the receiver to achieve powerful breakthroughs. Prophecy has impact. It arises out of a solid prayer agenda. Too much spontaneity in prophecy will eventually lead us into a place of mediocrity. How would you upgrade your relationship with the Holy Spirit so that your prophesying can move to a higher level of intentionality?

- Humility is a prerequisite when we are seeking to move in the supernatural realm. We need grace to become a different person who has seen something more of God. We need grace to move to a higher level of purpose and intentionality. What must change in your approach to people and the church so that you can become much more purposeful with your gifting? What new area of prophetic impact is the Lord giving you permission to step into for your friends, neighbors, and members of your church?

WHAT CONSTITUTES IMMATURITY?

One of my mentors, Graham Perrins, once described some prophecy as "an empty thought passing through an empty head." Admittedly this was in the period 1979–1984, but it does still hold true in many places today.

What we love, we think about. What we wish to excel in, we practice. We rehearse, prepare, study, and train so that we can achieve excellence. Jesus is worth all our energy and zeal. Prophecy represents Him and therefore needs to be as exemplary as teaching, as superb as the best preaching, as outstanding as a quality prayer. Our communication must be excellent.

Immaturity cuts corners. It relies more on the spontaneous than the well prepared. It cloaks its lack of content with hype, showmanship, and sensationalism. The loudness of the delivery is open, not passion released but paucity disguised.

- Immature prophecy is unprepared, unrehearsed. It is off the cuff, low level, mostly spontaneous, and lacking in power and impetus.
- The Holy Spirit is a genius. He is purposeful, highly articulate, deeply intentional, and totally focused. *"I know the plans I have for you, declares the Lord. Plans for your welfare not your calamity, to give you a future and a hope,"* (Jeremiah 29:11). If we are still moving in prophecy the same way we started after several years, we are not growing or developing. We are moving backward.

All things grow. It is time for an upgrade. What was acceptable a few years ago is a sign of immaturity now!

- Describe how the intentionality of God makes you feel about yourself.
- Explain the difference in context, presentation, and impact between a specific prophecy and a general one.
- Define the current level of your prophetic gift and specify what you must do to upgrade it to a higher level.

AN ASSIGNMENT

Think of a person around your life at this time who may be going through a troubling period of life.

READ PSALM 126.

When God moves in our lives, it is like the stuff of dreams. The gospel is so good it is almost too good to be true. The Lord can turn every life circumstance on its head. Our testimony is always about His greatness. He only does great things.

To walk with Him is to smile, to laugh, to shout with the sheer joy of being alive and in Him. When we forget who He is for us, then we are taken captive by our circumstances. We become pioneers of anxiety, worry, fear, and doubt. We lose our peace as faith disintegrates. In times like this we must sow into the greatness of God. Take the tiny mustard seed of faith and plant it into the name of Jesus.

We have to sow in order to reap a harvest. The spirit-filled life is one of constant sowing. God is faithful and generous. He takes the little that we have and multiplies it so that a few fish sandwiches feed a multitude of people. We are never beaten as long as we can sow one more thing into His greatness. We always sow into our own future. God is so amazing in this regard. He loves us to reap. He loves to guarantee our future in Himself. When we sow, we partner with Him in the present, for our future.

Read the psalm and study it. Ask the Lord for His own perspective so that you can think what He is thinking.

- What is your friend going through at this time that is difficult for them?
- What do they need to see turned around in their own life?
- The rule of life in the Spirit is simple for moments like this. It is: "Whatever you need the most, be the first to give it away," i.e., if you are ill, go and pray for someone who is sick. Sow to the Spirit. If you are in debt, give some money to the poor in your community. Sow to the Spirit. If you are under attack, give a blessing to someone else. Sow and reap.
- How would you encourage your friend to believe in the greatness of God at this time?
- What words from the Father's heart would inspire them to stir themselves and sow to the Spirit?
- Everyone has seed. It is part of our relationship with God. The power does not lie in the amount of seed that we possess but in the incredible fertile nature of the soil in which we place it. That soil is God's goodness.
- How could you speak this prophecy out in such a way that it would stimulate your friend to action?

Think of your own life. Do you need to sow to the Spirit now, for your future? Take some advice. Never stop sowing. In hard times, sow more. Sow every day. Sow in every conceivable way. It is how to invest in your own future.

Now, write out a prophecy. Craft a word of life for your friend that will inspire, encourage, and stimulate them to reach out to the Lord with the little seed that they have.

Think about how you should deliver the word. The power of the spoken word creates an impact that breaks through every hostile barrier. Sometimes our hearts get surrounded by doubt, fear, and hopelessness. Prophecy has the anointing and the power to break down that wall. (See Jeremiah 1:9 & 10!) Prophecy has the power to build people in the Spirit and to plant new hope and faith in their life. The secret of that power lies in the way that you say the word. Always allow your heart to be touched and inspired by the word you have received for another.

- How would the Lord say it? Ask the Holy Spirit to empower you with the same intentionality.
- Choose the right moment and the right place. Don't make a big production of it and do not be too casual either. Choose a time when there are no distractions, if you can. Possibly take someone with you so that you can join faith and pray for them.
- Deliver the word properly with due consideration and respect but also with power. Record it on tape if you are able. Give them the written version at least. Often it is important to give them both.
- Think about yourself. Do you need to sow to the Lord?

FRUIT OF THE SPIRIT

"The fruit of the Spirit is love, joy, peace, patience, kindness, goodness, faithfulness, gentleness, self-control; against such things there is no law." (Galatians 5:22, 23)

- What is your biggest challenge in becoming Christlike at this point in time? Identify and explain.
- Which fruit of the Spirit will most help you in overcoming this obstacle?
- What particular fruit of the Spirit is the Father most wanting you to develop in these next twelve months?
- How will the development of this aspect of God's nature most help you to: (a) draw near to God in a place of intimacy? (b) be enabled to build better relationships? (c) become a better person in your attitude and approach to life? (d) be empowered to overcome the schemes of the devil? (e) develop a stronger prophetic gifting?
- Ask the Lord to give you a word of prophecy about one of the fruits of the Spirit. What would you say to encourage someone in this regard? How would you speak out a word of prophecy challenging someone to step up into one of the attributes of the Spirit? How could you match the content with the delivery and give a clear prophetic blessing?

For your advice, when you identify a fruit of the Spirit that the Father wants to develop in you in the next time season, then it is vital to understand the following life principle:

All your tests in the following season are allowed by the Lord to establish this particular fruit in your life. As you cooperate with the Holy Spirit and choose the fruit He has indicated, then every situation you encounter will only establish that attribute in your life by experience. It is not easy but it can be done!

CASE STUDY: MATCHING PROPHETIC DELIVERY WITH CONTENT

The delivery of a prophetic word must match its content. One cannot grab someone by the throat and prophesy love and peace; likewise, a prophecy about warrior strength cannot be properly prophesied in an airy whisper. The context must match the content.

Below are a few prophetic words I have given to individuals enrolled in my prophetic schools (I have changed the names for privacy reasons). In this exercise, read the prophetic word and answer the questions following it.

PROPHETIC WORD

Laura, I see a big bowl of water and a brick being dropped into the middle of it. It's caused a big splash and displaced the water. God wants to drop a huge dollop of love in the middle of your fear so that the fear will actually be shot out of your life. This is who God is. Perfect love casts out fear. Nobody is safe from that blessing.

ANSWER THE FOLLOWING QUESTIONS

1.   What is the crux (focus) of this word?

2.   What is the emotion and plan God has for Laura?

3.   What would be the best way to deliver this word? What tone of voice would be best to use? What body language and position should be used?

4.   After delivering the word, what would you pray over her?

When I find someone who is fearful, I get excited, because I know what God wants to do in the coming months. Instead of majoring on the problem of fear, I prophesy of the love of God, because we have the scriptural and experiential precedent of how God deals with fear. When God brings His love, it displaces fear. One casts the other out. The next few months are always incredible as God lavishes His love on the person. He is in the business of bringing His love in stronger and stronger ways.

LECTIO DIVINA

Lectio Divina (Latin for *divine reading*) is an ancient way of reading the Bible — allowing a quiet and contemplative way of coming to
God's Word. *Lectio Divina* opens the pulse of the Scripture, helping
readers dig far deeper into the Word than normally happens in a quick
glance-over.

In this exercise, we will look at a portion of Scripture and use a
modified *Lectio Divina* technique to engage it. This technique can be
used on any piece of Scripture; I highly recommend using it for key
Bible passages that the Lord has highlighted for you, and for anything
you think might be an inheritance word for your life (see the *Crafted
Prayer Interactive Journal* for more on inheritance words).

READ THE SCRIPTURE

*For even as the body is one and yet has many members, and all
the members of the body, though they are many, are one body, so
also is Christ. For by one Spirit we were all baptized into one
body, whether Jews or Greeks, whether slaves or free, and we were
all made to drink of one Spirit. For the body is not one member,
but many.*

*If the foot says, "Because I am not a hand, I am not a part of the
body," it is not for this reason any the less a part of the body. And
if the ear says, "Because I am not an eye, I am not a part of the
body," it is not for this reason any the less a part of the body. If the
whole body were an eye, where would the hearing be? If the whole*

were hearing, where would the sense of smell be? But now God has placed the members, each one of them, in the body, just as He desired. If they were all one member, where would the body be?

But now there are many members, but one body. And the eye cannot say to the hand, "I have no need of you"; or again the head to the feet, "I have no need of you." On the contrary, it is much truer that the members of the body which seem to be weaker are necessary; and those members of the body which we deem less honorable, on these we bestow more abundant honor, and our less presentable members become much more presentable, whereas our more presentable members have no need of it. But God has so composed the body, giving more abundant honor to that member which lacked, so that there may be no division in the body, but that the members may have the same care for one another. And if one member suffers, all the members suffer with it; if one member is honored, all the members rejoice with it.

Now you are Christ's body, and individually members of it. And God has appointed in the church, first apostles, second prophets, third teachers, then miracles, then gifts of healings, helps, administrations, various kinds of tongues. All are not apostles, are they? All are not prophets, are they? All are not teachers, are they? All are not workers of miracles, are they? All do not have gifts of healings, do they? All do not speak with tongues, do they? All do not interpret, do they? But earnestly desire the greater gifts. And I show you a still more excellent way. (1 Corinthians 12:12–31)

1. Find a place of stillness before God. Embrace His peace. Chase the nattering thoughts out of your mind. Calm your body. Breathe slowly. Inhale. Exhale. Inhale. Exhale. Clear yourself of the distractions of life. Whisper the word "stillness." Take your time. When you find that rest in the Lord, enjoy it. Worship Him in it. Be with Him there.

2. Re-read the passage twice. Allow its words to become familiar to you. Investigate Paul's word picture of the body. What images does that bring to your spirit? What do you see? Become a part of it. What phrases or words especially resonate with you? Meditate especially on those shreds of revelation. Write those pieces down in your journal.

3. Read the passage twice again. Like waves crashing onto a shore, let the words of Scripture crash onto your spirit. What excites you? What scares you? What exhilarates you about this revelation of the nature of God? What are you discerning? What are you feeling? What are you hearing? Again, write it all down in your journal.

4. Write the theme of this passage in your journal.

5. Does this passage rekindle any memories or experiences? Does it remind you of any prophetic words you have given or received? Write those down as well.

6. What is the Holy Spirit saying to you through this scripture? Investigate it with Him — picture the two of you walking through it together. Write those words in your journal.

7. Read the passage two final times. Meditate on it. Is there something God wants you to do? Is there something He is calling you to? Write it down.

8. Pray silently. Tell God what this passage is saying to you. Tell Him what you are thinking about. Write down your conversation together. Picture yourself and the Holy Spirit as two old friends in a coffee shop, chatting about what God is doing.

9. Finally, pray and thank God for His relationship with you. Come back to the passage once a week for the next three months. Read it and let more revelation flow into you. If you feel compelled to,

craft a prayer based on this passage for yourself, your family, your friends, or your church. Pray that prayer until you feel God has birthed it in you.

A RELATIONAL VALUE

- Do not merely treat this value as an exercise but as an opportunity to develop Christlike intent for yourself.
- Develop this value into a prophetic word in order to demonstrate the importance of your ministry arising out of your relationship with the Lord.
- Read the scriptures out loud several times.
- Think through the introductory paragraph and the main points.
- Work through the Action Points 1–8.
- Improve the Value Statement and make it your own.

This exercise can be done by individuals or groups of 2–4 working together using dialogue. This guide is understated deliberately to allow for wide-ranging thinking or discussion.

A group should be able to take the concept further in dialogue.

Follow up the action points with each other and get personal feedback from everyone regarding their progress.

NON-NEGOTIABLE LOVE

SCRIPTURES

John 15:9

Romans 12:10

Colossians 3:12–17

1 Corinthians 13:1–7

1 Peter 4:8

There is nothing we can do to make God love us more, and there is nothing we can do that would make Him love us less! His love is based on who He is within Himself, not on our performance.

He is consistent and faithful in how He loves us. His love is never on the negotiating table when we are in dispute and disrepute with Him. How can we be anything less for each other?

His love enables us to be true to one another when we have difficulties. Keeping His way of loving in the forefront of our minds in times of complexity helps us to be true to God in the way that we hold on to one another.

- Love means being patient and expressing kindness.
- Love does not remember slights, hold grudges, or recall bad history.
- Love is unselfish and thoughtful.
- Loving people bear all things well and believe the best of others.
- Truly forgiving and forgetting is the hallmark of God's love in us.
- Love is not provoked and foregoes vengeance.
- Love never fails.
- Be devoted to one another in brotherly love.

- Love is an action, not just a word.
- Real love allows people to change.

ACTION

1.   Think of someone recently where you have not fully been the loving person the Holy Spirit was expecting you to be in the situation—and be reconciled.

2.   Take time to thoughtfully upgrade your love with the people around you.

3.   Using the above scriptures and comments, develop a word of prophecy on the theme of God's love.

4.   Who is the intended target for this word?

5.   How would you deliver it in a way that fulfilled the objective?

6.   Record the word in writing or on tape.

7.   Deliver it to the person concerned.

8.   Write an evaluation of the process and result.

VALUE STATEMENT

Non-negotiable love is being the best expression of Christ to another human being. Putting love first and last in every situation keeps us in the abiding presence of God.

Non-negotiable love can heal and seal every problem that may occur in any relationship.

A LIFE PRINCIPLE FOR PROPHETIC MINISTRY

We must pursue our calling within a working structure of intentional relationships. This process will inevitably on days revolve around being purified, moving in loving confrontation, and the discipleship necessary to enable each one of us to grow up into all things in Christ. Cultivating values and principles in how we use our gifting will enable us to be proactive in our own development into a place of freedom and maturity.

We are all responsible for our own behavior. We are answerable to the Lord and to one another in the improvement and expansion of our gift and calling.

This life principle if followed will enable us to understand and experience the personality and character of the Lord Jesus as it relates to moving in the gift of prophecy.

THE NATURE OF GOD

SCRIPTURES

Exodus 34:6–9

Matthew 5:43–48

John 13:34, 35

Philippians 2:1–13

2 Thessalonians 3:5

1 John 4:7–21

All of life is an exploration into the secret place of God's heart for humanity. The Father is extremely intentional toward not only His own people but also all mankind.

Prophetic people proclaim who God is for people. In order for those words to be authentic, they must be backed up by our experience of His essential nature in our own lives.

"The testimony of Jesus is the spirit of prophecy" (Revelation 19:10). We prophesy from the same place of revelatory insight as our current experience of God. We all have a testimony of what God is like to us on a consistent basis. Our mouth speaks of what our heart knows to be true.

God is good. He is loving, kind, generous, and compassionate. He does not lie, so what He says about Himself is the whole truth and fit for prophecy. He is everlastingly unchanging and consistent. He is good news. Prophecy is the proclamation of the steadfast nature of God.

Therefore the way that we move in the gift of prophecy must be consistent with His name and nature.

What we think about God is the most important issue in the world to us (see Matthew 16:15).

- A true perspective on God's nature is essential in our prophesying.
- It is important then that we upgrade our image of God within our own hearts.

ACTION POINTS

Answer as many questions as you need to!

- What is your current picture of God? Write it down in 4–6 sentences or phrases.
- How long have you had this image? Is it time for an upgrade?
- Is your image biblical? Can you put scripture(s) alongside it? Do so!
- What do you need to change?
- What do you need God to be in you in this current season?
- Sit quietly, relax, and ask the Holy Spirit to give you a vision of God for this next season. Keep persevering until the whole picture emerges *and* your faith begins to rise and worship flows.
- What scripture can support this image?
- What is the Spirit saying to you through this picture and the word?
- How can you become this image of God to the people around you? What must change in you?
- Now keep this picture alive through praise and worship!

Principle: I must discover the nature of God for myself and develop that revelation into an actual relationship experience.

I must only prophesy out of that place of internal relationship and truth.

A PROPHECY: DISCOVER IDENTITY AND INHERITANCE

THIS NEXT TWELVE MONTHS YOU will see the glory of God in your own life, in your own circumstances. I will cause you to rise up and occupy a place of overcoming. You shall overcome yourself, that you will no longer be your own worst enemy. When you have conquered yourself, then I will send you out on a great adventure. Nothing will overwhelm you because I will teach you that every obstacle is indeed an opportunity and every opposition can be laid low. That which will rise up in you in this next twelve months will be nothing less than the sovereignty and the declared majesty of your God. It is My intention, says the Father, that you would know Me, that you would be strong, and that you would do exploits. You would be filled to overflowing with the goodness of God, that you would know the majesty of God, that you would have the joy of the Lord. The power of God will overshadow you and erupt within you. You will no longer be the person that you once were but I will turn you into a different man and a different woman. Then, says the Lord, we will really get on with the business of the living Father.

This next twelve months, it's for you to discover who I am for you. It's for you to come to a place of trust, a place of peace, a place of rest, and a place of faith. It is for you to discover who I am for you and as your Father. I intend to enjoy myself this year because during this year you will actually stop whining. You will begin worshiping and that will be good for My ears. I intend to enjoy Myself, beloved. In this next twelve months, I want to bring you into a place where your life is a joy and a delight to yourself, where you will enjoy your life and you will be delighted with your life and you will be ecstatic about who you are becoming. I will banish low self-esteem. I will do violence to self-hatred. I will bring you into a place where you are happy and relaxed about who you are because when I look at you, I'm happy; I'm relaxed. You are not much of a challenge to Me, says the Lord. I know you are amazing but you are not much of a challenge to Me. I can beat you with My little finger. You are not much of a challenge. I will do something so compelling, so wonderful that I will make you a challenger against the enemy for the rest of your life.

My intention is for My glory to cover the earth as the waters cover the sea, to have multitudes of people covering the landscape of nations to reveal My presence to a hurting world.

The art of practicing My presence is to pay attention to My character and My nature. This is reflected in righteousness with grace; holiness plus mercy; spirit and truth; and wisdom and revelation. Practicing presence depends absolutely and resolutely on engaging with the fruit of the Spirit in everyday circumstances with people around you.

People who are nice, difficult, oppositional, hateful, obstinate, mean, loving, judgmental, bullying, spiteful, and vindictive—all these are the means by which I will teach you to become like Me.

To be able to rise up, you must become humble. To live above your circumstance, you must know the real stance in every circumstance. Loving Me and loving others is the major requirement of the kingdom. When you love you release goodness.

I will take advantage of every negative relationship to teach you how to live in the fruit of the Spirit, to practice unity and oneness with us.

In less controlled situations where you are tempted to cut corners and settle for something less, I will show you my integrity, honesty, and purity of life and purpose so that you may live from a place of honor.

I do not give shortcuts, but to those who desire fullness, I provide a quickening spirit, on My terms. Children have the promise of inheritance but must grow up into a place of competency so that the gift of God is not squandered.

I am so willing for you to receive all that My Son died to give you. You must be willing to come into the place of development and continual practice with the Holy Spirit.

There are two things happening, beloved. First, you are learning to trust Me in all your life sitations. You are practicing the joy and peace in believing when things are against you.

Second, we are watching over you to determine when we can trust you with what we most want to give you. A son or a minstry can only release into the world what they have actually received by relationship and obedience.

What you do in ministry must be authenticated in your relationship and fellowship in the kingdom.

This is your time to taste and see that I AM good. It is a culminating season of growth, opportunity, and experience of the Holy Spirit as your Helper.

He will lead you into all truth. You are moving in identity toward inheritance. You have found favor in My sight. Now you must see it and know it by experience so that we can elevate you to the place of heritage and fullfillment.

RECOMMENDED READING

Title	Author	Publisher
Hearing God	Dallas Willard	InterVarsity Press
The Gift of Prophecy	Jack Deere	Vine Books
Surprised by the Voice of God	Jack Deere	Zondervan
Growing in the Prophetic	Mike Bickle	Kingsway
The Seer	James Goll	Destiny Image
Prophetic Etiquette	Michael Sullivant	Creation House
The Prophets' Notebook	Barry Kissel	Kingsway
User Friendly Prophecy	Larry Randolph	Destiny Image
Prophecy in Practice	Jim Paul	Monarch Books
Can You Hear Me?: Tuning in to the God Who Speaks	Brad Jersak	Trafford Press
When Heaven Invades Earth	Bill Johnson	Treasure House
Knowledge of the Holy	A. W. Tozer	O. M. Publishing
The Pleasures of Loving God	Mike Bickle	Creation House
Manifest Presence	Jack Hayford	Chosen

Title	Author	Publisher
Living the Spirit-Formed Life	Jack Hayford	Regal
The Agape Road	Bob Mumford	Lifechangers
The Sensitivity of the Spirit	R. T. Kendall	Hodder & Stoughton
Living in the Freedom of the Spirit	Tom Marshall	Sovereign World
Secrets of the Secret Place	Bob Sorge	Oasis House
The Heart of Worship	Matt Redman	Regal
Experiencing the Depths of Jesus Christ	Jeanne Guyon	Seedsowers
The Unsurrendered Soul	Liberty Savard	Bridge-Logos
Keys to Heaven's Economy	Shawn Bolz	NewType
Translating God	Shawn Bolz	NewType
Growing Up With God	Shawn Bolz	NewType
God Secrets	Shawn Bolz	NewType
Breakthrough, Prophecies, Prayer & Declarations	Shawn Bolz	NewType
Exploring the Prophetic; 90-Day Devotional	Shawn Bolz	NewType
Modern Prophets	Shawn Bolz	NewType
Your Prophetic Life Map	Steve Witt	Emanate Books

ABOUT THE PROPHETIC EQUIPPING SERIES

Graham began teaching prophetic schools in 1986. Eight years later he wrote *Developing Your Prophetic Gifting*, a book that has won universal acclaim. Translated into numerous languages, reprinted many times over, and published by several companies, it has been a best seller and widely regarded as a classic. Graham has continued to develop new material each year in the Schools of Prophecy. Now after almost twenty years of teaching continuously upgraded material, the School of Prophecy has developed into one of the finest teaching programs on the prophetic gift, ministry, and office of a prophet. This new material effectively makes *Developing Your Prophetic Gifting* redundant.

The Prophetic Equipping Series is an ongoing writing project that combines classic teaching with the journal format so popular in the Being with God series. It also embraces training assignments, workshops, and reflective exercises, with emphasis on producing one of the finest teaching aids on the prophetic gift and ministry. These manuals are appropriate for individual, small-group or church-wide use. All Christians can prophesy and would benefit from Graham's wisdom and experience in ministry. The assignments, exercises, workshops, *lectio divina,* and other material are designed to further the understanding of the prophetic gift, ministry, and office. If used properly, the process will develop accountability for prophetic people, healthy pastoring of the prophetic, and give relevant questions for leadership and prophetic people to ask one another.

ABOUT THE AUTHOR

Graham Cooke and his wife, Theresa, live in Santa Barbara where they quide and interact with several communities that are millennial, entrepreneurial, and focused on the city.

Graham has a leadership and consulting role in a variety of groups and organizations at regional, national, and international levels. He is a mentor to ministries and works in various think-tanks to promote kingdom initiatives.

Theresa has a passion for worship and dance. She loves intercession, cares about injustice and abuse, and has compassion for those who are sick, suffering, and disenfranchised.

Together they have two sons, three daughters, and eight grandchildren! They also have two other daughters in Australia who are part of their extended family.

Graham is involved in three aspects of ministry, each of which has a business model attached. These are:

BrilliantPerspectives.com—the consulting and training group that produces a range of messages across the spectrum of life in Christ, church development, and kingdom engagement.

BrilliantBookHouse.com—the online resource for the physical and digital production of all Graham's messages, conferences, and school series, plus all his books and propheitc soaking words that have had a profound impact on individuals, families, and churches around the world.

BrilliantTv.com—our online streaming platform with thousands of subscribers receiving constant, consistent discipleship training and personal development input through a curated online community that is worldwide.